A Short Guide
to Writing

A Short Guide to Writing

✦ ✦ ✦

Steven Lynn
University of South Carolina

Allyn and Bacon

Boston   London   Toronto   Sydney   Tokyo   Singapore

Vice President, Humanities: Joseph Opiela
Editorial Assistant: Kate Tolini
Marketing Manager: Lisa Kimball
Production Administrator: Annette Joseph
Editorial-Production Service: Holly Crawford
Text Design and Electronic Composition: Denise Hoffman
Composition Buyer: Linda Cox
Manufacturing Buyer: Suzanne Lareau
Cover Administrator: Suzanne Harbison

Library of Congress Cataloging-in-Publication Data

Lynn, Steven
    A short guide to writing / Steven Lynn.
      p.   cm.
    Includes index.
    ISBN 0-205-18934-2
    1. English language—Rhetoric. I. Title.
PE1408.L93   1997
808'.042—dc20   96-30523
                            CIP

Printed in the United States of America
10 9 8 7 6 5 4 3 2 1   01 00 99 98 97 96

For Mike and Lisa
and
Ben and Leora

Contents

✦ ✦ ✦

◆ 3 *Drafting*   61

◆ 4 *Finishing*   83

Part Two
The Workshops

Preface

✦ ✦ ✦

If you're looking for a long, intricate, formal, exhaustive discussion of how to improve your writing, you've clearly picked up the wrong book. But, of course, no one, except maybe an obscure sect of masochistic Zoroastrian monks, is looking for such a thing.

What I think you *are* looking for is a clear and lively guide to all the different kinds of writing you might encounter both in school and work. You're looking, I hope, for useful tips on understanding different writing tasks, on generating, arranging, and organizing your ideas, on revising and editing. You'd like to be able to write with confidence, knowing from the start that you'll likely be able to succeed at any reasonable writing assignment, knowing also that your writing won't embarrass you grammatically or logically. About grammar and usage there are many superstitions, and you'd no doubt like to be able to separate the pseudo-rules from the real ones. You'd probably like to expand and enrich your stylistic options, and you'd like some solid advice on handling research papers and in-class essays. And you'd like all this as concisely and efficiently as possible.

If that's what you're looking for, then put your feet up and keep reading. (If you're one of those aforementioned monks, I suggest you try Lord Kames's eight-volume *Elements of Criticism*.)

The confluence of great writing teachers in my life is suspicious—almost an Argument from Design itself. I've benefited greatly in many ways from Karl Beason, the world's greatest high school English teacher; Donald Greiner and George Geckle, my undergraduate idols; John Trimble, James Garrison, and James Kinneavy, my graduate school gurus; and Carolyn Matalene, my colleague in Composition and Rhetoric at the University of South Carolina and unofficial mentor. Other colleagues who have helped me understand how writing is nurtured include Nancy Thompson, Tom Waldrep, Rhonda Grego, William Rivers, and Patrick Scott. The hundreds of teaching assistants whom I've worked with over the last 14 or so years have also taught me much, and I thank them. They almost always acted as if I knew what I was doing, which helped inspire me to figure it out. And I'm especially indebted to all of my students: without them, teaching writing would be impossible.

Without the vision and encouragement of Joe Opiela, my editor at Allyn and Bacon, this book would still be a bunch of handouts, notes on a napkin, an abandoned manuscript, and some disorganized electrochemical energy. I also want to thank all those reviewers who so generously contributed suggestions and appreciation: Paul Heilker, Virginia Tech; David Jolliffe, DePaul University; James McDonald, University of Southwestern Louisiana; and Twila Yates Papay, Rollins College. I've drawn extensively on their ideas. Many thanks to Holly Crawford, my astute copyeditor, and to Denise Hoffman, who designed this book. I'm also indebted to Jennie Ariail, our extraordinary Writing Center Director, for her help with the research chapter. My administrative assistants, Elizabeth Smith and Robbie Bell, and my various research assistants, Dyanna Phillips, Chris Miller, Denise Wolitz, and Randall Miller, have assisted in many capacities very effectively and with good cheer.

Finally, I must acknowledge here the patience and inspiration of my best and toughest audience, Annette, my wife, and Anna, my toddler. I know that this short guide isn't nearly short enough, and it is seriously lacking in pictures, but I did my best.

I would also like to acknowledge my most excellent brother and sister, Mike Lynn and Lisa Schimpf, and my wonderful parents, Ben and Leora Lynn, to whom this book is dedicated. They have always been islands of sympathy and good cheer, and they are much appreciated.

1

Before

*Words are like money; there is nothing so useless, unless
when in actual use.*

— Samuel Butler (*Notebooks*, 1912)

You can skip the first section of this chapter if you're already completely fired up about improving your writing. But if you have any
doubts at all that you are embarking on one of the most important
endeavors of your life, or if you just want to see if I've thought of
any reasons why writing is important that you haven't, then do
have a look here at this first section. The second section of this
chapter offers some important insights into why writing is so difficult, which leads into the third section, which considers how to
make writing easier—and more effective, too.

Why Writing Is So Important

The average college student changes his or her major three times;
hence, any course might determine your career, and all of them
will likely change your life in some way. But, any course that

focuses on writing has a special importance. In fact, one could argue that writing, for a number of reasons, is probably the second most important subject you will study, whatever your major.

Surprising? Consider, for starters, how much writing you'll need to do when you graduate. Engineering majors (at least some of whom chose engineering partly because they did not particularly enjoy literature and composition) can plan to spend roughly a fifth to a fourth of their time writing. An engineer, in other words, can expect to spend about one day a week writing. People in most other fields probably spend as much, if not more, time "composing" in some sense—reports, letters, memorandums, speeches, talks, instructions, complaints, responses, inquiries, and all sorts of other things.

Further, as you gain responsibility and rank, the importance of your writing will increase. If you think that you'll be so rich and powerful that your secretary can do all your writing, or at least clean up whatever you scribble out, then you should think again. Writing is a powerful tool; you'll want to be able to wield it yourself. The way you say something is often as important as what you say. If someone else controls your writing, then that person controls your image and your effectiveness.

Plus, writing is much more than polishing up preexisting ideas. Rather, writing is in itself a way of learning, a mechanism for discovery and for thinking things through. Thus, the clarity and imagination that are needed in writing apply to your personal as well as to your professional life. Most of us often solve our biggest problems by talking things over with a friend. Writing allows you to talk things over with yourself, to express your ideas in private, and also to record them in a way that makes possible more precision and detail than most people can manage in conversation. Of course, writing is also important for your success in college, and its importance increases as your level of education increases.

You may have begun reading this section with some vague idea that, yes, writing was fairly important, and, yes, you would like to do well in your English classes. But writing is actually crucially important: It is not an exaggeration to say that it is very likely one of the keys to your success and perhaps even your happiness.

Why Writing Is So Difficult

Perhaps the most important thing beginning writers should know (and we are all beginning in some sense) is that writing well is not easy, even for the best professionals. If writing *is* easy for you, then at least one of two things is true: You are a great genius, blessed with an uncanny ability to express ideas; or you're not doing it right. Occasionally, to be sure, a writer will find a patch of smooth-running water and the prose will slide right across it effortlessly. More often, the writer faces cross-currents, eddies, rapids, under-tows, and gashing boulders; concentration and sustained effort are needed. And I'm not talking about some hotshot writer who's working on the Great American Novel. I'm talking about anyone— the writer who's just trying to write a memo that has to convey a good bit of information and coax the cooperation of various people without confusing or irritating anyone; the writer who's trying to persuade the city council to widen the street somewhere else; or the writer who's trying to explain all the complexities of feeding and caring for the horses and sheep while the owner is out of town.

Why does writing of all sorts often seem as difficult as negotiating a twisting mountain river? I see two reasons, both of which are important for you to know about:

1. *Writing is not natural.* Children learn how to talk by observing other people talking and then imitating them. Although we may encourage children to talk, we generally don't teach them in any formal way. Talking seems to come naturally. But learning to write generally calls for more explicit and extensive instruction. Writing is an invention—more difficult in some important ways than speaking—employing complexities and multitudinous con-

ventions of committing language to paper (or stone, monitor screen, billboard, sky, or whatever). You shouldn't feel discouraged if you find writing difficult and complicated. *It is*. It is, perhaps, the most amazing thing human beings do.

2. Writing is also difficult because it usually demands more coherence, care, and thoroughness than speech does. When we talk with someone, we have many clues other than the words themselves to tell us what is meant; we have, for instance, tone, facial expression, and body language. Most people would rather conduct important business in person for just this reason. A writer can't necessarily tell where a particular reader will be confused, unconvinced, or bored, and so the writer has to try to anticipate what various readers may want at any moment. Good writing, to be sure, often sounds like speech—without all the repetition, delays, wandering around, and feedback that make up talking. But to remove everything we don't need to make sense, and to add all that we do—that's hard work. Textbooks that tell you writing is easy, that it's not mysterious, and that they have surefire methods that always work—well, those people probably believe they can reverse baldness by unclogging hair follicles.

Still, with the difficulty of writing comes also considerable pleasure. As Barbara Tuchman has said, "Nothing is more satisfying than to write a good sentence." "Nothing?" you might be thinking. "*Nothing?*" Well, let us just say, *very few* things are more satisfying, and perhaps Tuchman should get out a bit more. At least, difficult as writing is, almost everything that is more satisfying than a good sentence costs considerably more trouble and expense. (Now if Tuchman had said "a *great* sentence" . . .)

How to Make Writing Easier

There are reasons to wait until the very last minute to begin any writing task: you may enjoy the adrenalin rush of panic and anxiety; you may want to avoid wasting effort in case you are hit by lightning and don't have to turn in the assigned paper; you may be trying to flunk out of school in order to begin your work career immediately; or something else.

There are also reasons to start as soon as possible—to begin writing immediately when an assignment is given. Obviously, the sooner you start, the more time you will have, but this initiative does not necessarily mean that if you start sooner, you will have to do more work. In fact, the contrary is likely to be the case.

How's that? How will starting sooner make for less effort and yet a better result? Everyone, I suspect, has tried in vain to solve a problem only to realize the answer when the whole problem has been set aside. How did the solution suddenly occur when you were taking a shower, playing tennis, standing on the sidewalk, thinking about nothing in particular? The solution occurred because your unconscious mind continued to work on the problem, even while your conscious mind went on to other things.

So, if you will engage your mind in the assigned task as soon as possible, you can then go for a walk or a movie and still have some part of your brain working on the project—as if you had hired some cowriters. If you start early enough, you will also be able to work in small chunks of time, staying fresh and taking breaks.

However, a certain amount of delay and procrastination is perhaps almost inevitable in almost every kind of writing. If you have the time to waste, you'll figure out how to waste it. Almost everyone's mind naturally resists hard labor. As Newton said, objects at rest tend to stay at rest. But if you can get your mind in motion early, you will find your delays and daydreams are often productive; as Newton also said, objects in motion tend to stay in motion. Get your mind in motion as soon as possible, and you'll find yourself picking up speed and momentum as you go along. And don't worry too much if your mind wanders off while you're trying to write. That happens to everyone. Indeed, such daydreams may lead you to useful ideas. Just keep returning your attention periodically to the task at hand, and keep those ideas rolling.

Although it might seem obvious that to write one should seek out a quiet, well-lighted place without distractions, interviews with writers and self-reports suggest otherwise, surprisingly enough. Some writers work accompanied by music or even the television; some like to have their children playing around them; others like to sit in a restaurant or cafe. I know of two detective story authors who meet almost every morning at MacDonald's and write together for several hours in their regular booth. Some research has, in fact, indicated that people tend to concentrate better with some background noise, perhaps because the noise forces them to focus more intently on the task.

In other words, you should not think you need to wait to write until you're in the library, or until your roommate is gone or asleep, or until you've solved every other problem that might distract you. Good writing has been done under just about any circumstances you can imagine. (The Gettysburg Address, legend has it, was written by Abraham Lincoln on the train on the way to his speech.) You will likely find, of course, that some circumstances work better than others for you, and most writers do like to work in the same place with the same materials, if possible. The point here is not only that you want to find out where you write best, but also that you don't want to be too fussy about it. You can probably write anywhere if you put your mind to it.

What materials do you need to write? Thomas Wolfe supposedly used the top of a refrigerator to write on while standing up (he was tall), and Mickey Spillane has written sometimes in his boat with his typewriter on his knees. Parts of this book (I won't tell you which ones) were written at a beach house on various scraps of paper found around the house. While in prison, the Marquis de Sade wrote entire novels on a few pieces of paper, using microscopic handwriting. Thus, just about any materials will do. But it is, to be sure, easier to build a brick wall with a brick mason's trowel and a tape measure, than with a kitchen knife and a yardstick. And if you have a choice, a computer with a good word-processing package is—for most people—definitely the tool of choice for writ-

ing. Because a computer makes it so much easier t
down, to move them around, and to delete portion
many students find themselves adopting the sort of ¡
exploratory stance that is especially useful in drafting a piece of
writing.

But if you're not yet on-line, remember that a computer is not
necessary to write well or even quickly. Long before the advent of
disk drives, Anthony Trollope and Samuel Johnson were able to
write thousands of well-crafted words in just a few hours. You can
still put ideas down, move them around, delete them, revise them,
whatever, the old-fashioned way—with scissors and tape, ink and
typewriter. In fact, some writers who have worked at a computer
for years still find that particularly difficult passages require them
to compose with pen and paper.

In addition to a computer, other luxuries worth attending to
include good lighting, plenty of neat workspace, and a comfortable
chair. As far as the materials needed to write well, however, you really only need something to write with and something to write on.

If you're writing an in-class essay, or an essay exam, you probably have little choice about the time, place, or materials. But the
basic principles of writing nonetheless apply. Even writing in class,
under severe constraints of time, you should still give yourself
some time for planning and thinking. If you start writing immediately, without brainstorming, the odds are high that your first few
sentences will be the intellectual equivalent of clearing your
throat: as you write, you'll be figuring out what you're going to say,
what angle you're going to take.

Although we can assume that teachers ordinarily read their
students' papers all the way through, we must realize that in-class
essays are likely to be treated differently: the teacher is attempting,
usually, to see what you know about something, and he or she is
attempting to place your response into some letter-grade category.
Thus, your reader may be disproportionately impressed or depressed by your first few sentences, and it therefore may be even
more important with in-class essays than with other kinds of writ-

ing that you start strongly. A little preparation can go a long way. Even if you only have twenty minutes to write an in-class essay, spend two or three minutes thinking and planning; then you'll have fourteen or fifteen minutes to write furiously, and two or three minutes to read over and edit your work.

Finally, here are a few simple but very useful tips that will help make your writing go more quickly and more smoothly. These may seem like minor, even trivial, matters but they're worth considering.

✦ *Some Basic Tips*

- First, give yourself room on your drafts to make corrections and revisions: always skip lines, whether you are writing by hand, typewriter, or computer; and employ one-inch margins on all sides. You might even triple space sometimes. It is difficult and even irritating to try to revise and rethink when all the space on the page is already covered with writing.

- Likewise, if you write by hand, use only one side of the page. Your writing will be more legible, as well as being easier to cut and paste.

- Indeed, do anything to your draft pages that will make the job of putting your manuscript together faster and easier. Too many students treat their manuscripts with reverence and are reluctant to cut and paste, strike out, insert, tape together, and so forth. When you are famous, of course, your manuscripts will be precious—but they'll be much more interesting if you've actually worked on them!

- Make copies of your work, anticipating and thereby avoiding disaster. Just about everybody smart enough to operate a computer knows you should save your work often (every fifteen minutes at least), make back-up copies, and print out hard copies regularly. But it is very easy to forget about the fallibility of machines and assume the power won't suddenly go out, or the hard drive crash, or the disk go bad.

- By the same token, retain copies of any papers you turn in. Teachers, as a rule, don't lose student papers, but life is full of accidents. Ernest Hemingway apparently lost an entire book manuscript, leaving it in a taxi in Paris. Although it is some trouble (if you don't have a personal copy machine) to make copies, it is certainly much easier than recreating a paper or a book.

2

Beginning

It's appropriate to pause and say that the writer is one
who, embarking upon a task, does not know what to do.

—Donald Barthelme (1985)

It could be somewhat comforting to read this chapter's epigraph. As Barthelme suggests, if you don't know what to do when you begin a writing task, you are in good company. Still, knowing you're among all the best people as you stand on the deck of the tilting Titanic provides rather limited consolation. Fortunately, your writing ship is not going down, for the writer, as Barthelme might have gone on to say, is also one who knows what to do in order to figure out what to do: namely, to put it most succinctly, he or she writes.

The present chapter elaborates considerably on this always amazing process of analyzing a task, thinking of things to say, and giving them some form. By understanding these three crucial activities better, you'll be better able to float just about any writing project safely into the harbor.

Let's look first at analyzing the task.

Kinds of Aims

What is going on when a writer is working? What questions could we ask to get some idea of what the writer is doing? These seem fundamental to me:

> What are you writing about?
> To whom are you writing?
> Why are you writing?
> How are you writing?

These questions seem fundamental, as rhetoricians from Aristotle to James Kinneavy have indicated, because they reflect different and essential aspects of the work of writing: the subject (What?), the audience (To whom?), the writer (Why?), and the style (How?). (See Figure 2.1.)

Although any particular piece of writing unavoidably involves all the elements of writer, reader, subject, and style, it is nonetheless useful to think about writing in terms of these different emphases or aims. That is, we can think about how the writer, the subject, the audience, and the writing itself are figured into a text; we can think of a particular piece of writing as emphasizing the writer, or the subject, or the audience, or the writing itself. As

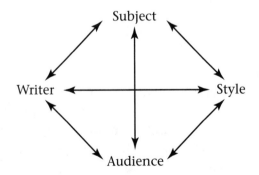

◆ **Figure 2.1**   Aspects of the Work of Writing

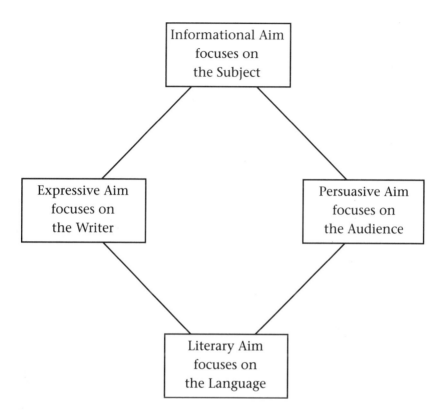

✦ **Figure 2.2** Aims in Writing

shown in Figure 2.2, the emphasis on the writer's self-expression can be called an *expressive* aim; the focus on conveying information about a subject can be called an *informational* aim; an emphasis on affecting the audience can be called a *persuasive* aim; and a focus on the language itself can be called a *literary* aim.

Expressive Writing

Genuinely introspective acts of writing, in which the writer is essentially motivated only to express himself or herself, without regard for subject, audience, or style, rarely appear in print. Such expressive writing most often appears in private spaces, usually in what most people would call a personal journal. The power and pleasure of such unfettered self-expression and exploration is suggested simply by the large number of people over the centuries who have kept such journals. If you've never kept a journal before, you owe it to yourself to start one. Use it as a place to meditate on life, to muse over your schoolwork, to draft some lines of poetry just for yourself: write anything you like. You may be surprised how your writing ability improves simply by writing regularly about things that matter to you.

If self-expressive and exploratory texts usually remain private, they are nonetheless often the starting point for more public documents, as the writer discovers useful and important things to say while talking to him- or herself. To see how easily self-expression shifts to other aims, compare the following pairs of writing tasks:

1a. How do you feel about the increase in tuition?
1b. Explain to the university president how you feel about the increase in tuition.

2a. What is your reaction to the congressional pay raise vote?
2b. Tell your congressman how you react to the recent vote to increase congressional pay.

3a. What do you think of the movie version of *Twelfth Night*?
3b. In a review for your student newspaper, explain what you think about the movie version of *Twelfth Night*.

Notice in these examples how simply adding an audience moves the assigned writing from expressive toward persuasive writing. And it's easy enough to see how the task could be more precisely defined as a persuasive purpose: "Write a letter in which you attempt to convince the university president either to stand by the decision to raise tuition or to reverse the decision."

In fact, sometimes assignments that seem to be asking you to express yourself really mean for your expression to include conveying information or constructing an argument. Consider who is going to read your writing and what the audience's purpose in reading your work will be. If you have any questions about an assignment, take advantage of any opportunity to ask for clarification. If you determine that the assignment is actually an invitation for you to express yourself, then here are a few suggestions that you may find helpful.

✦ *Tips for Expressive Writing*

- Recognize that in expressive writing, many sentences are likely to begin with "I." The topic may shift unexpectedly, as one statement sparks another, and the writer's feelings and attentions shift. One statement may contradict another one as the writer discovers his or her own conflicting insights. (By contrast, in writing that focuses on something other than the writer's own consciousness, the sentences are more likely to begin with words that name the subject being considered; the topic is unlikely to shift unexpectedly, since the writer's attention is supposedly fixed; and contradictory statements are likely to be avoided or resolved, since the writer is presumably attempting to make some clear and coherent sense of the subject.)

- Most issues of any importance are complex, sparking conflicting emotions. If you anticipate a reader (other than yourself) for your self-expression, you might want to indicate that you recognize any contradictions that emerge.

(continued)

- Give yourself plenty of time to explore your feelings; allow yourself a chance to see what you think, to develop your response. Starting early is always a good idea, but especially so with self-expressive writing.

- Strive for honesty. If your teacher has assigned an expressive essay, she or he should really want you to reveal yourself.

- Explain the basis of your feelings. You can better understand your feelings and ideas if you understand how you came to have them. Illustrations and/or examples should be helpful, even if you're writing for yourself.

Informational Writing

One of the most common writing assignments in school and work is to convey information. With such a task, your job is to sift through material and determine what your audience needs to know, then package that information in such a way that your audience can most effectively grasp it.

One obvious consideration is vocabulary. What terms does your audience need to understand? What ideas or concepts require explanation? And how can you explain them? Sometimes writers try to explain some specialized term or concept by using the vocabulary of the specialty. That's fine, if the audience does, in fact, consist of specialists. If not, then the unfamiliar needs to be explained in terms of the familiar. It would be easy for a physicist to explain how powerful the Hubble telescope is to other physicists: he or she could simply say, "It has a magnification power of 8.3^{100}." But that doesn't mean anything to most people. Notice how Robert

Zimmerman explains Hubble's power in terms anyone can understand by using a simple comparison:

> Take this magazine outside and tape it to any convenient lamppost. Now get into your car and start driving. It will help if you live in, say, Kansas or Nebraska, where you can pretend the earth is flat, the air is clear and the roads go pretty much in a straight line. When you have gone about 600 miles, get out of the car, turn around and try to read the headline at the top of the page.
>
> Not easy, eh? That, however, is exactly what astronomers have just done with the refurbished Hubble Space Telescope.
>
> —*The Sciences*, March/April 1996

Beyond using familiar terms and revealing comparisons, what other basic tips for conveying information can be given? Imagine that you've been asked to inspect Squishy Tennis Balls, a manufacturing plant, and report back to your Board of Directors. Read the following excerpts from two different versions of that report, and think about how they differ. As a board member, which would you rather read? Which conveys information more clearly and efficiently?

VERSION 1
Squishy Tennis Balls Report

Tom and I arrived at 8:15 and met the assistant manager, John Roberts, who showed us around the main office. We noticed that every workstation had both a computer terminal and a typewriter, but most of the secretarial staff were using typewriters (approximately 10 of 16 were working at typewriters). Mr. Roberts confirmed that most of the staff were uncomfortable with the computers. We inquired about the details of the computer system, which was installed about two years ago for about one million dollars. It is a very powerful system. We then had coffee in Mr. Roberts's office while we waited for the manager, Robin Shealy, to arrive. After twenty minutes, Mr. Roberts said Mr. Shealy was sure to get there any minute, but he suggested we begin our tour of the plant.

We went from the main office to the loading dock and met Mark Taylor, the foreman. Mr. Taylor was clearly upset by our visit because a truck had arrived to unload some raw materials at the same time that a truck was still being loaded with an outgoing shipment.

We left the loading dock and went to the finishing room. Mr. Shealy joined us in the finishing room and sent Mr. Roberts back to the main office. Mr. Shealy informed us that Mr. Roberts had told him we would arrive at 9:00.

[The report goes on for six more pages.]

VERSION 2
Squishy Tennis Balls Report

In general Tom and I found that the plant is producing a good product, but it is not operating as efficiently as it should. Two problems need to be addressed immediately.

Computer Usage

Although the plant was outfitted two years ago with a powerful central computer system, one that is still very nearly state-of-the-art and cost us almost one million dollars, the use of this system is minimal. The computer obviously can improve communication between and within departments greatly: we saw confusion over the time of our visit, the loading of trucks, the storage of extra supplies, and much else (see below).

Only the sales department relies on the computer for important tasks. The other departments rely on typewriters, hand-written notes, and verbal communications. Even planning calculations are done by hand. Personnel in all the departments, especially maintenance, shipping, finishing, and preparation, should be trained to take advantage of the computer system.

[The report goes on for six more pages.]

As you can see, the first version is a story of what happened, in chronological order. In some situations, such a narrative is what your audience wants, without your ordering of the material. The audience simply wants you to be a verbal videocam, reporting what you've experienced. Most of the time, however, such an orientation is what John Hayes and Linda Flower call "writer-based"; little packaging for the reader has been applied.

The second version required the author to organize the material for the audience, thinking of what they would want. It could be called "reader-based" because it is oriented toward the reader's needs, not the writer's. The board wants to know, the author presumes, if any action needs to be taken based on the visit, and the author has accordingly imposed an order on the information. Instead of having to pull out the important information from the stream of what happened, readers already have the information organized for them.

Are there other tips for conveying information effectively? Yes: every piece of advice in this book, really, will potentially help you convey information, for anything that improves your writing makes you a better communicator. Clarity and comprehension are not necessarily the only virtues in informational writing, for the writer still has to consider whether the audience *wants* this information. If the writer looks out and sees an audience with little or no interest in the subject, or even an antipathy toward it, then the task of writing shifts toward the realm of persuasion, for the audience has to be moved to want to receive the information being conveyed. So, let's have a quick look at persuasion as an aim. But first, here are the tips we covered specifically for informational writing:

✦ *Tips for Informational Writing*

- Use terms and concepts the reader understands, or explain any unfamiliar terms and concepts that are essential.

- Explain the unfamiliar in terms of the familiar. Use comparisons.

- Arrange the information for the convenience and comprehension of the reader.

- Avoid distracting features (grammatical errors, intrusive humor, stylistic flourishes, for instance).

- Make relationships and transitions explicit, showing the reader how particular facts and points connect.

- Support generalizations or abstractions with examples and illustrations.

Persuasive Writing

When the writer's main goal is to *persuade* the audience to adopt (or reaffirm) a particular position, then conveying information becomes part of a strategy to influence the audience, a means to an end rather than an end in itself. Although clarity and thoroughness may be crucially important in conveying information, other values would seem to be paramount in persuading.

Audiences are persuaded by three factors: their perception of the author; their feelings about the message; and their understanding of the argument's logic. The audience's perception of you as a persuader will be based on many things besides the substance of your main point, including your word choice, sentence structure, apparent reasonableness, and your anticipation of what the audience already knows and feels. Obviously, poor grammar or obscure wording won't help convince the audience that your ideas are worthy of acceptance. Failing to present your ideas in the appropriate format won't score you any points either. In sum, your self-presentation becomes a strategic part of how the argument itself will be received.

You also need to consider how the audience already feels about what you want to argue. We sometimes imagine that we live in a world in which arguments are evaluated on the basis of the facts, but in actuality the facts themselves may be perceived differently by different audiences. Although pure logic alone may sway any Vulcans in your audience, most human readers are influenced by emotional appeals. If you want to be successful as a persuader, you'll need to consider where the audience is starting from emotionally as well as intellectually, and how they will feel about what you want to say.

But sheer emotion will sway only the most shallow and uninformed audiences; you will also want to consider the logic of your argument and how that logic will appeal to your audience. What will your audience accept as reasonable evidence? What use of that evidence will they accept? If your evidence is based on medical research, or government statistics, or personal anecdote, or historical documents, for instance, how will your audience respond to that kind of evidence?

Let's say you're going to argue to the PTA (Parents and Teachers Association, a school support organization) that football should be downplayed and soccer emphasized. Your audience will first want to know who you are and how you, as a person, are related to your position. Are you a maker of soccer equipment? Are you some crusading nerd fanatic who's really against all sports? Or, are you an experienced soccer player? Are you swept away by emotion, or have you really thought this thing through? Have you been involved in the PTA before, or did you just pop up for this issue? If you explain, for instance, that you're a parent of children who are choosing whether to play soccer or football, and that you're also a former football player, then the audience might likely be receptive to what you have to say. Of course, you can't change who you are; but you can certainly change how you present yourself.

How about the audience? Who are they? How will their character affect your argument? Imagine, for instance, that you are addressing parents in a rural town in Texas. It seems reasonable to assume that many of them would be football fans; some probably have played football—the men mostly, although some women may have played flag football or frontyard football at least. It's also likely that some of them have little understanding of soccer, although soccer is certainly much more popular today than it was ten or twenty or thirty years ago, when the audience was growing up. Emotionally, they're unlikely as a group to have any deep or personal affection for soccer—although certainly there may be huge exceptions. In some cities with a strong immigrant tradition, St. Louis for instance, soccer has been established as a strong youth sport for at least a couple of generations. As you can see, thinking about your audience—how they feel, what they know, how they will perceive you—is crucial.

How could you affect those emotions? You might point out how enthusiastic fans are about soccer worldwide and how easy it is to understand soccer. You might show a videotaped clip of an exciting moment in a World Cup match. You might point to the difference in injury rates for soccer players versus football players: that should be a particularly effective emotional strategy for parents.

Finally, you'll want to consider what evidence and logic this audience will value. For instance, in a rural town in Texas, which has probably been focused for decades on high school football in the fall, facts about the popularity of soccer around the world probably won't carry too much weight. Your audience may not be that interested in becoming more like the rest of the world. Facts about the relative costs of running a soccer program versus a football program might influence a rural Texas audience somewhat, but that's probably not a clinching argument. Facts about how many children can't participate in football, but could participate in soccer, would be more persuasive, I suspect. You might well conclude that you want to say little or nothing directly against football, stressing instead support for soccer. You certainly wouldn't want to start by attacking football, for that would tend to antagonize your audience before you've had a chance to present your position.

Indeed, to persuade an audience, you will find it very useful to establish some kind of common ground with them. According to Carl Rogers, an influential psychologist (whose ideas were introduced into writing instruction by Maxine Hairston), a good first step in any disagreement is for both parties to demonstrate they understand the opponent's position. If you and I disagree, in other words, I wouldn't be allowed (by the rules of Rogerian argument) to argue my case until I had proved to you that I at least understood your position, even if I didn't agree with it.

Although you probably don't want to begin every persuasive effort with a thorough presentation of the opposing position, Rogerian thinking can be very useful in the process of writing an essay. By trying to state fairly the opposite of what you want to argue, you are likely to see more clearly what points you need to concede and what points you need to counter. You're also likely to think of more support for your own position.

While the formal study of logic can be helpful in analyzing and constructing arguments, your brain is already naturally set up to think reasonably. The biggest logical problem most people have in arguing is that we don't use our good common sense. Consider for example this beginning of a student essay on a heated topic:

> We, as women, often hear about someone having an abortion, if not ourselves. We consider this the "easy" way out of our responsibilities and problems; well, it's not. We seem not to realize that having an abortion can be detrimental. The damage an abortion can cause is not only physical, but mental.

Is this paragraph reasonable? As the opening to a persuasive paper on an emotional and divisive issue, is it effective? Advanced training in logic is not required to see that there are problems here. The writer states, speaking apparently for all women, that we "often hear about someone having an abortion." Is that true? How does the writer know that all women often hear about someone having an abortion? If "often" means, say, once a day, or once a week, I suspect many women would disagree.

This questionable claim merely raises the topic of abortion, and it is not logically connected to the second assertion, that women consider abortion the "'easy' way out of our responsibilities and problems." Again, how does the writer know that all women consider abortion to be an easy way out, or for that matter that some women do not realize "that having an abortion can be detrimental"? This type of logical flaw is quite common, especially in an early draft: the writer here is apparently generalizing about a whole group based on an awareness of a small part of the group. She assumes that her own experience, and perhaps the experience of her friends, exemplifies every woman's experience.

Such an error is, in fact, so common it has a familiar name, *hasty generalization*. Fortunately, it's easy to fix. In evolving her paper, the writer simply needs to examine her conclusions, asking specifically if they really do apply to the group that is named. Compare the logic of this revision to the original:

> All too often I hear about someone having an abortion, and I naturally assume that these women believe an abortion is the "easy" way out. They must believe, at least, that having an abortion is easier than having a child. Such a decision neglects to consider, however, that an abortion can cause not only physical, but also mental, damage. There is no easy way out of an unwanted pregnancy, but I believe there are better choices than abortion.

The revision is more logical and persuasive because it does not make claims that are overstated. It also makes a connection between the two assertions that abortions are common and that women believe abortion to be an easy way out. In the original, a reader might see the first two statements as being only loosely related, not logically connected. If your reader can't make some connection between your various points, then the points are not likely to promote your argument. This lack of connection in an argument is also so common a logical flaw that it has retained its Latin name; it's called a *non sequitur,* which means "it does not follow."

There are lots of other ways to be illogical: one might try to discredit or dismiss a point by attacking the person who's making it (that's called an argument *ad hominem,* or "against the person"); one could introduce an irrelevant but interesting point to distract attention from the facts (such a point is called a *red herring,* after the practice of dragging a herring across the trail of prey to confuse hunting dogs); one could *argue in a circle,* drawing a conclusion that is really already part of the starting point ("abortion is bad because it is wrong"); one could assert that one event caused another one, when actually the two may be unrelated—*post hoc ergo propter hoc,* it's called—which means, "after that, therefore because of that" ("As soccer has become more popular, drug use among teenagers has increased," for instance); and many more.

Obviously, you want to avoid such logical fallacies, but no one will be persuaded by what is missing from an argument. Turning these fallacies around does suggest the sort of evidence that will be persuasive. In drafting an essay, for instance, you're looking for plausible generalizations, not "hasty" ones. You want to make claims that your evidence will support, qualifying with "perhaps," or "I believe," or whatever, as necessary; you want to show your evidence clearly to the reader. What is plausible depends, of course, on the audience—on what they will understand and accept. Likewise, instead of *non sequiturs,* you want an argument that is linked together: not only do you need to see how you get from one point to the next, but also you need to be confident that your audience can see it too. Instead of circular reasoning, you want your argument to evolve. If certain assumptions are crucial to your argument, you need to explain those assumptions or be reasonably certain that your audience shares them.

As you can see, in persuasive discourse, everything depends on the audience—how they will perceive the writer, how they will react emotionally to the argument, how they will perceive the evidence.

✦ *Tips for Persuasive Writing*

- Starting points are especially crucial in persuasion. If you can begin with some kind of common ground, you've got the best chance to lead an audience to other insights and opinions.
- In selecting evidence, consider what your audience already knows and believes.
- Present yourself persuasively. Indicate that you are informed, organized, clear, fair, principled—that you are, in short, the sort of person we should listen to and perhaps agree with. Obviously, grammatical errors, which are often distracting in conveying information, may be fatal to your case in persuading simply because they undermine your credibility.
- Use an engaging style to make your case convincingly and compellingly. (Pages 83–103 deal specifically with style.)
- Use plausible logic. Avoid fallacies and overstating your case.

Literary Writing

A writer may also focus mostly on the language itself, on the way something is being said. Such an emphasis does not mean that a poet or novelist avoids having a subject or affecting an audience or expressing ideas and feelings. But a good work of literature, we usually feel, is more than just what it means: if the words were changed, the work itself would be impoverished. We appreciate the text itself, as well as what it says and does.

If your teacher asks you to write a poem, a short story, or even a play, don't panic. You can do it. You can, in fact, enjoy it. Just follow the same procedure you'd use for writing anything else. (The third section of this chapter discusses how to get ideas.) Don't sit around waiting for inspiration to strike. Although some writers have endorsed the idea that creative literature comes magically in flashes of insight, these same writers seem to produce multiple drafts with careful rewriting. Most creative writers say they don't know what they're going to say until they say it, and even those who plan extensively also alter their plans extensively. Virtually all creative works are driven in some sense by conflict, so that's what you want to discover: what are the opposing forces in your work?

The main thing is to let yourself go: enjoy what you write, generate lots of material, and be prepared to throw away a lot of it.

You may know from the start what form you're going to work in—sonnet, realistic short story, open verse, science fiction—or you may find that the form naturally evolves in the process of writing. In any event, if you possibly can, spend time reading the sort of thing you want to produce. Then set those works and any other preconceptions aside, and enjoy yourself. All writing, after all, is creative.

Kinds of Structure

If you were in London and someone told you to drive to Bath, it's unlikely that you would immediately hop in a car and start driving in whatever direction seemed best. Instead, you would consider where you wanted to go, and where you were, and map out a course from here to there. Then you'd start out, adjusting your route as the trip developed and road conditions, weather, and other factors emerged.

But many students do the compositional equivalent of hopping in and driving off when given a writing assignment. Imagine a student in an American History class who is given the following assignment on an in-class essay exam:

Discuss the causes of the Civil War.

This is not a particularly exciting or imaginative assignment in itself—but there is also nothing to prevent you from getting excited about it or using your imagination. Admittedly, some writing tasks are more immediately inviting than others; but to write well, you'll want to figure out how to make the task your own—that is, how you can feel committed and enthusiastic about it. The American Civil War is an incredibly fascinating event, and this question really allows you to deal with its causes in whatever way you see fit. If the topic is boring, ultimately it is your own fault (and you, I know, are not a boring person). Even if the assignment asks you to discuss the mating habits of newts, you can adopt a stance, a way of seeing, that makes the subject interesting. (What, indeed, makes for a sexy newt?)

Most teachers, in my experience, say that the fundamental problem of student writing is a failure in some way or other to carry out the assigned task. How can you zero in on what you're supposed to do as a writer? Even when the assignment is open, and you can write about whatever you like, it should be helpful to think about how to analyze the task you are giving yourself. To understand how to structure your writing, you need to understand clearly what you're trying to accomplish. I suggest you consider three aspects of any task: the verb, the topic, and the audience.

The Verb

Every assignment should have a verb that names the action—and hence implies the structures—your essay should employ. If the verb is "discuss," then you have less guidance, and more possibilities, than you would with some others. "Discuss" could mean just about anything, from "talk about for a while" to "analyze" or "compose" or "support" or "refute" or something else. Whenever you encounter "discuss" (and it is frequently used), or any other verb for that matter, you need to consider what you're really being asked to do. Let's think for a moment about some of the verbs more commonly used in assignments.

Agree or Disagree.   Assignments that ask you to agree or disagree may seem to imply that one response is correct and that you should pick one side or the other. Oftentimes, however, a good case can be made either way, and the teacher genuinely wants you to think for yourself. The important thing, usually, is not whether you actually agree or disagree, but how well you support your position. Thus, you shouldn't assume that your position has to be simple; few issues, examined carefully, really are simple. So, even if you essentially agree (or disagree), you should also acknowledge the good points of the opposing position, while also explaining why those good points are outweighed. (If they aren't outweighed, then maybe you should reconsider your position.) "Discuss the causes of the Civil War" could be approached by presenting one authority's explanation of the causes and then agreeing and/or disagreeing with that accounting.

Analyze.   In assignments that ask you to "analyze x," the activity involves breaking the object of attention, the "x," into its parts. Often there will be at least one *obvious* way to take apart and display the "x," but this strategy may not necessarily be most effective. For instance, if you were asked to analyze a Volvo 940 sedan, you might naturally break it down into the engine and drive train; brakes and tires; seating; sound system; and so forth, explaining each part. But let's imagine that the audience for your analysis is a potential buyer of a Volvo 940, then your analysis might proceed differently—into, say, value, safety, durability, reliability, and so forth. You could treat "Discuss the causes of the Civil War" as an "analyze" assignment by breaking down the different kinds of causes.

Classify. An assignment that asks you to "classify" is, like an "analyze" assignment, asking you to organize data. A classification system groups related items together on the basis of shared traits. Let's say you were to list all the classes at a particular college or university. That would be quite a list, numbering in the hundreds, perhaps thousands. If someone were to ask you what courses are available at that school, other than reading the entire list to them, which would take hours, what could you say? Clearly, you'd need to organize the classes into groups—into classes. This classification of classes would allow you to deal with the unwieldy complexity of all the individual classes. That's the purpose of classification: to help us make sense of the world by organizing it.

What would your classification of classes look like? The different groupings might look a lot like the various departments on campus, allowing you to say, "There are English classes available, plus Psychology, Math, Biology, Chemistry, Physics, Music, Theatre, History, and Political Science." But such a classification, natural as it may seem, is not the only way to organize the data. You might divide the classes differently and tell your friend, "We have large lecture, small lecture, discussion, and laboratory classes." Or you might say, "We have classes on the old original campus, classes held on the new east side, and classes at the coliseum complex." The nature of your response depends on the basis of your classification: subject matter, size, place, or whatever.

In using classification, you need to watch out for a few things. First, a common problem is using an inconsistent basis of classification. You don't want to divide classes into "large," "English," and "at the coliseum." Second, try to make the classification complete. If you're classifying by place, for instance, what about those classes that take place electronically via television? They don't fit into the existing classes; therefore, at least one more class is needed. Third (related to the previous point), it is acceptable for classes to have only one member. However, if you have very many classes like that, the classification may not be very helpful in organizing the data. Likewise, classes with huge numbers of members may not be very revealing.

Do keep in mind that the categories and the bases of classification are constructed by you, the classifier. Some groupings may seem more natural, but classes are made by humans. It may make sense to most people to group Biology and Chemistry in the same category, but there may be some purpose for which Psychology and Biology, or Biology and Philosophy, actually make more sense together. Like everything in writing, the way you classify depends on your purpose.

You might well find, pondering the Civil War, that there were so many particular causes that it's difficult to comprehend them. So you might then want to classify them into related kinds of causes, say economic, social, and political. The way you group the causes together (as with analysis) should depend on both your own logic and your purpose in classifying, which is a powerful intellectual tool.

Compare and/or Contrast. Like the other methods of organizing information considered here, comparison and contrast is more than a way of shaping a paper. It is a fundamental strategy of the human brain. It is difficult—perhaps impossible—to imagine how we could understand or know anything in isolation, apart from anything else. You know what an apple is because you know it fits into the category "fruit." It isn't a rock, an animal, or another person, or lots of other things. We can compare an apple to other fruits and find that, yes, an apple is one of those. (It is, in fact, easy enough to compare apples and oranges.) We can identify the object in front of us as an apple, however, because we can also distinguish it from other fruits. Without the ability to compare and contrast, we could not make sense of the world.

Comparing looks at how two or more entities are similar, and contrasting examines how two or more entities are different. Comparison and contrast thus take a static view of what is being compared or contrasted. Although it may seem natural to compare or to contrast certain features, it is, again, important to remind yourself that you select which aspects to compare and contrast.

What you select and how you arrange your material depends, as always, on what you're trying to accomplish, but it may be helpful to consider that you have two basic options. Say you're comparing and contrasting a Ford Taurus and a Volvo 240. You could discuss a feature of one, then the same feature on the other car. Then take another feature, and compare and contrast it. And then another. Or you could discuss all the features of one car, then all the features of the other car.

The advantage of the first strategy is that the reader can see most clearly how the two compare and contrast. The potential problem is that the reader's sense of each item as a whole may be obscured. So, if you choose this structure for comparison and contrast, you will want to be sure to remind your reader of the overall picture. The advantage of the second strategy is that the reader gets a clearer picture of one item as a whole, but the weakness is that the reader may not see as clearly how the points compare to each other. So, if you choose this arrangement, you may want to refer back to #1 as you discuss #2, linking the two together, especially if the points of comparison are numerous or complex.

Although some guidebooks will tell you to be sure your comparisons and contrasts are balanced, giving roughly equal time to both #1 and #2, real writers often emphasize one item or the other, using comparison and contrast to make a point (and not as an exercise in proportion). If you'll keep in mind what you want to accomplish, it will usually be clear which pattern will work best.

Consider How. These kinds of assignments ask you to explain the development of an entity, as in "Consider how the Civil War began." How is this assignment different from "Discuss the causes of the Civil War" or "Analyze the causes"? Although these tasks are clearly related, "Consider how" usually suggests a chronological orientation, implying you should trace a sequence of events (rather than classify the kinds or analyze the different factors).

Define. In explaining the causes of the Civil War, you might decide it would be useful to define just what a "civil war" or a "cause" is. How would you do that?

A formal definition is usually presented as having three components:

A = B minus C.

A is the entity being defined; B is a category into which A falls; C refers to the features that differentiate A from B. For instance: "An Olympic gold medal is an award given to an athlete." In this definition, A is "An Olympic gold medal," the thing being defined; B, the category being used, is "an award"; C, the differentiating feature, is "given to an athlete," distinguishing this award from others. This definition would be useful to someone who didn't know what an Olympic gold medal is, but we might think about how it could be adapted to be more effective in particular situations.

First, consider the category. Ideally, the thing being defined will be placed into a category that is familiar to the reader. If I am told that "a swardlarp is a kind of kahoti," I'm not any better off. If I'm told that "a swardlarp is a kind of stew," then the definition is helpful. So, you will want to keep in mind the following tip:

• *Make sure the category is familiar.* Certainly, "an award" is familiar. But how helpful is it? Is the gold medal just any award? The category here is very large, and it would be more helpful if it were more specific. Likewise, "a kind of stew" is helpful, but "stew" is still a large category. If we said "an Iranian beef stew," then the reader's idea comes into much sharper focus. So, we need to add the second tip:

• *Make sure the category is specific enough to be helpful.* The Olympic gold medal is not just "an award." It would be better to say it is "an award given to the best athlete in a particular event in the Olympics," thus differentiating it more effectively.

Obviously, a category can be made too specific or detailed in the wrong way to be helpful. Consider: "A gold medal is an award made of molded gold, weighing fourteen pounds, four inches in diameter." This statement is true, and for certain purposes, it would be an excellent definition—which brings us to the third tip:

• *Shape the definition to your purpose.* If someone wants to know what swardlarp is in order to make it, then an effective definition should include the ingredients. If someone wants to know what to do with it, then saying it is "an Iranian beef stew served only on New Year's Day" would be an effective definition, whereas listing the ingredients wouldn't.

When you are writing an argumentative essay that is based on definition or expanding an argumentative paper by using definition, you're obviously doing more than supplying a dictionary definition. Then you are *arguing* for a definition. But the strategy for defining is essentially the same. If you want to argue that the gold medal is a symbol of the competitiveness that blocks cooperation among nations, you will need a category (a symbol of competitiveness) and differentiating characteristics (your explanation of the kind of competitiveness).

Words mean, as Humpty Dumpty said, whatever we choose to make them mean. That's the power of definition.

Describe.   You might believe that an effective description is necessarily one that overwhelms the reader with details, but such is rarely the case. An effective description is instead one that serves its intended purpose, so the place to begin when you are describing is with this question: Why am I describing this person, place, or thing? Do you simply want to experience the object of your attention more fully, or are you attempting to inform or persuade the reader?

Let's look, for example, at a descriptive passage from Eudora Welty's *One Writer's Beginnings*. Welty has been talking about a trip she and her father made by train, and she talks here about the drinking cup her father carried along:

> In Daddy's leather grip was his traveler's drinking cup, collapsible; a lid to fit over it had a ring to carry it by; it traveled in a round leather box. This treasure would be brought out at my request, for me to bear to the water cooler at the end of the Pullman car, fill to the brim, and bear back to my seat, to drink water over its smooth lip. The taste of silver could almost be relied on to shock your teeth.

Welty's description is, you will notice, detailed: The cup had a lid with a carrying ring; it was collapsible; it was made of silver, and traveled in a round leather box. But there is much we are not told about her father's drinking cup. (What were its dimensions? How many collapsible segments did it have? Was it scratched up? Shiny? What was its shape? Its origin? How large was the carrying ring? And so on.) Welty's purpose is not to convey a complete description of the cup, but rather to create a certain impression that is useful to her larger aim. Later on, Welty tells us that the train trip opened up a dreamworld to her imagination, as she invented what lay beyond the paths, roads, and rivers they passed; and her father "put it all into the frame of regularity, predictability," and "that was his fatherly gift in the course of our journey."

Thus, Welty's effort to give the reader information about her father's drinking cup contributes to the idea that his presence helped control and channel her imagining. She offers a description of the cup that gives some sense of it as a tangible thing, but we do not need to see it fully. We just need the impression of this cup as one aspect of the father's "regularity, predictability"—he always had this useful cup. We can imagine the rest.

Although writers may well encounter situations when an exhaustive description is appropriate, most descriptions, in fact, are like Welty's: they are evocative. In order to convey an impression to your readers, you just need to select those details that serve your purpose. In using description to develop a piece of writing, you will probably rely most on the sense of sight. Linguists have observed that languages invariably contain more vocabulary for conveying visual impressions than any other sense. But don't overlook the value of using the other senses in your description: touch, smell, taste, hearing. Welty's passage strikingly mentions "the taste of silver," and suggests the shocking touch of the silver against her teeth, along with its smoothness against her lips.

Although a rich vocabulary is helpful in description (and virtually any other writing task), you may notice that Welty's description does not rely on uncommon words. The key to an effective description is careful observation and selection, not a fancy vocabulary. If you do not know the word *azure,* you can nonetheless convey the picture you want: "Her eyes were the color of an unclouded sky." In fact, such comparisons are oftentimes powerfully effective. Here is another passage from Welty:

> Sometimes the encroaching walls of mountains woke me by clapping at my ears. The tunnels made the train's passage resound like the "loud" pedal of a piano, a roar that seemed to last as long as a giant's temper tantrum.

The two comparisons in this brief passage make the description of the sound of passing through the tunnels memorable: the sound is amplified as if a "loud" piano pedal has been depressed; the sound lasts as long as a giant's temper tantrum. That's wonderful writing.

Thus, effective description depends on patience and imagination. You need to be patient enough to observe carefully what you are describing (even if the observation is in your mind) and to select those details that serve your purpose. Even a brick, carefully and imaginatively observed, can yield a very rich description, making part of the world vivid and impressive to your readers.

Evaluate. To evaluate involves comparing one thing to another or comparing one thing to an ideal. If an assignment directs you to evaluate two different explanations of how the Civil War came about, your response will naturally attempt to see which explanation better accounts for what happened. An ideal explanation would account for every fact, so you would not only be comparing one explanation to the other, but you would also (at least implicitly) be comparing each explanation to a hypothetical ideal one. Again, take care in such assignments that you don't oversimplify, offering only positive or only negative comments.

Narrate. A narrative is a story: this happened, and then this happened, and then this. We use stories, of course, for various purposes, and (as with description) it's crucial for you to consider the purpose your narrative will serve. Are you simply trying to entertain the reader? Are you using an anecdote to support a point? Are you explaining how something happened or providing a progress report for a supervisor? Are you narrating the steps one needs to take to do something successfully?

If, for example, you are attempting to entertain your reader, the most effective way to tell a story may be to begin with your standing on the stage, looking out at a crowded theater, dressed in a toy soldier's uniform, even though the story (as you see it) really begins the summer before, when you decided, on a dare, to enroll in a beginning ballet course. Fiction often begins in the middle of things, or at the end, and these are appealing and underused techniques in nonfiction. If your purpose, however, is to explain the steps involved in carrying out a task, then you probably want to start at the beginning and go through to the end. Conveying information clearly, not engaging the reader's attention and interest, is your top priority in that case.

Look at this extraordinarily lucid and engaging narration of a complicated biochemical process and consider what this scientific narration, by Robert Wallace, has in common with Welty's descripton:

> In the cell's manufacturing district the messenger RNA turns into an intricate assembly line. Small organelles called ribosomes slide along its length like miniature tape players, reading each set of coded instructions, or codon. The codon's message is simple: "Bring me an amino acid"—one codon, one amino acid. What fetches the amino acid is a fleet of RNA molecules known collectively as transfer RNA. One end of a transfer RNA molecule, called the acceptor stem, lassoes amino acids out of the cellular cytoplasm; the other end, known as the anticodon, is keyed to plug into the codon. When the ribosome reads a codon, a piece of transfer RNA shunts into place, bearing the specified amino acid. Then enzymes weld the amino acid onto the previous link in the growing protein chain.
>
> —*The Sciences*, March/April 1996, p. 10

Wallace's comparisons here, the careful and creative choice of words ("assembly line," "miniature tape players," "lassoes"), the use of drama (bringing the codon to life, letting it speak)—even the punctuation and syntax—all contribute to making this narrative convey information very effectively.

Even your selection of the events to present should be affected by your purpose. If you are explaining a particular movement as an example of how difficult ballet is, then standing on the stage before a performance may not be an essential event. But if you're expressing how it feels to dance publicly for the first time, then that momentous event seems very important.

As you develop writing by narration, also keep in mind that time can be divided up in various ways: one "event" may be better seen for some purposes as three separate events, or it may need to be combined with other activities into one larger event. The story of a wedding may involve "taking the vows"; or the event may be simply "the ceremony"; or taking the vows may be discussed as "my vows" and "his vows," or in many other ways.

However you decide to order and organize your narrative, you should keep in mind the following:

• Keep your reader oriented with such time markers as "then," "and next," "later," "first," "at the same time," and so forth. Be explicit about the time relationships of the various events; what is obvious to you, may be fuzzy to someone else.

• Pay attention to your verb tenses. There's no rule against using different tenses in the same paragraph, or even sentences, as many students seem to think. The following sentence, for instance, is perfectly fine:

He knows she will think that he had slept there. But he had learned long ago that a woman in love will often believe what she wants to believe.

• A good story has conflict—a hero and an antagonist at least. Even though you may not immediately think of your narrative as a story (perhaps you are explaining the process of growing turnips or narrating what you did on your first date), it will often be helpful to conceive it in those terms. By thinking in terms of a story, for instance, you may be better able to decide whether an event should be included. Is it part of the plot? Does it illuminate the hero or the opposing force? You may even be sparked to consider what the opposing force might be in a particular narrative.

• Give some thought to the point of view of your narrative. From what position is the story being told? How does that position affect the telling of your narrative?

• Finally, in narrative as in all other things, quotations can be very effective. Almost always, getting some dialogue into a narration can be engaging. Readers like to hear people talking (or even places or things talking, as in the case of Wallace's codon, if that seems appropriate).

A particularly important kind of narrative deals with cause and effect, another essential pattern of organizing. Whenever you attempt to explain how something happened, you're engaging in cause and effect analysis. As a structural pattern, cause and effect structures often begin at the end of the story, with the effect, and work backwards to the cause of the ending—but not necessarily.

When you use cause and effect patterns to develop a piece of writing, it's a good idea to be cautious about assigning causes. It may seem obvious to you (to take a simple example) that your sister has tooth decay because she eats a lot of candy. But the causes of events really aren't ever so simple as they may seem. There are people who eat lots of candy and have no tooth decay. Perhaps your sister has tooth decay because she eats lots of candy and does not floss and brush as she ought to. Still, there may well be people who eat just as much candy, floss and brush just as poorly, and yet do not have the tooth decay your sister has. So perhaps a cause of the effect of your sister's tooth decay is also her personal tendency to have cavities. Perhaps her teeth just don't resist decay as well as some other people's.

At this point, you may be wondering about the feasibility of using cause and effect at all. It is, indeed, always tricky. But we have to do it. If your experiment fails, your airplane is late, or your best friend is mad, you want to know why. So, we do the best we can. The important thing is not to limit your attention to one cause simply because it seems obvious.

You should give some thought to remote causes as well as to the more obvious and immediate ones. Eating candy and not brushing would seem to be linked rather directly to getting tooth decay. Such nearby causes are often termed *proximate*. Having a genetic make-up that is susceptible to cavities is a somewhat more distant cause, contributing to the effect, but not causing it in itself. An even more remote cause might be the evolution of the human diet, which brought refined sugar into our mouths rather late. One could argue that since early humans ate nuts, fruits, and vegetables, teeth simply haven't yet evolved to deal with candy.

How do you know whether a particular analysis should include more distant causes? Look to your purpose. Your sister's dentist, explaining why she has so many cavities, probably won't want to talk about the evolution of human teeth. The dentist's interest is probably in the immediate causes, the ones that your sister can do something about. But let's say the dentist senses that your sister is upset and depressed by the assessment of her teeth. It might be helpful to include in the explanation the more distant cause, reassuring your sister that it's not totally her fault, that other people also have trouble with tooth decay because teeth really haven't been designed for the foods people eat today.

Of course, you should also keep in mind that your understanding of a particular cause could be entirely wrong. It's possible that the candy isn't the problem at all, but rather the culprit is peanut butter, or milk shakes, or something in the water, or even a misdiagnosis in determining that there is decay. In assigning causes and identifying effects, you're always on slippery footing, whether you realize it or not.

Persuade. Occasionally an assignment may ask you to persuade your reader. If a particular audience is designated, then consider carefully their assumptions. If you want to argue that the cause of the Civil War was economic, not social or moral, in nature, your argument would likely be presented differently for the Sons of Confederate Soldiers and for the National Association for the Advancement of Colored People (NAACP).

Refute or Support. These tasks call for the same strategies as agree-or-disagree.

Summarize. Ideally, with any assignment, you'll be able to select which information to use, which to leave out. If you're forced to employ every bit of information that you can possibly think of on a topic, then you may not have studied deeply enough. Successful summaries necessarily omit some information and elaborate on other features; thus, the student is required to demon-strate an understanding of a topic by intelligently shrinking or omitting some parts of it while expanding upon others.

The Topic

It's a good idea to circle the noun or noun phrase that names the subject of the assignment. Notice any qualifiers or specifiers. If the assignment says "discuss the causes of the Civil War," for instance, then it's obviously crucial to focus on the *causes*, not just Abraham Lincoln's role or the Civil War in general.

The Audience

Here's one assignment: "For an issue of the *Weekly Reader*, read by sixth-graders across the United States, write a discussion of the causes of the Civil War." Here's another: "In a speech to the Daughters of the American Confederacy, discuss the causes of the Civil War." Obviously your discussion for these two audiences would be substantially different. The *Weekly Reader* audience would require background information that the Daughters would not; the Daughters might want justification of some points that other audiences would readily accept. The vocabulary and wording would be different. If you believe that Southern antebellum culture nurtured an independent spirit that sometimes became an arrogant im-morality, you'll need to be careful how you put this opinion to avoid offending the Daughters or confusing the sixth graders.

For many writing tasks, however, it is hard to know who your audience might be. Readers of a major newspaper, magazine, com-pany newsletter, or investment report would have widely varying levels of prior interests, abilities, and motivations. But classroom assignments are also often especially tricky because the audience is often unclear for a different reason: if no audience is designated, are you supposed to write for the teacher? If you do think of the teacher as the only audience, then you're often in the odd position of giving the audience information it already possesses. Ordinarily you'd be careful to acknowledge this prior awareness, saying "of course," "obviously," "as you know," and such. Readers usually don't mind some exposition of things they already know, as long as they know that you know that they know. Otherwise, they wonder if you're really speaking to them or to some other less-informed audience. But should you acknowledge that the teacher already possesses the information you're conveying?

Usually the best strategy in classroom writing is to imagine an intelligent reader who is uninformed on the particular assignment topic, but is well-educated otherwise. You will be aware, of course, that your teacher *is* the audience in the end, but you are not trying to communicate exclusively with him or her; rather (unless you're told otherwise), imagine that the teacher will be judging your ability to communicate with an uninformed reader—and not your ability to repeat information to someone who already has that information.

Perhaps the best advice anyone can give you about analyzing a writing assignment is this: When you're not sure what to do, ask for clarification. If that is not possible, then consider building into your discussion an explanation of how you interpret the task and what you are trying to do, thereby revealing to your reader that you did consider carefully what to do and providing some insight into your uncertainty.

Ways of Thinking

Scene one: You're staring at a blank area of screen or paper where words should be appearing, but they aren't. You check the time. It's getting late. You're hungry. (But didn't you just have a whole bag of M & M's?) You're thirsty. (Hey, you just drank a big glass of water.) Okay, you're sleepy. (Uh, you just had a ten-minute "refresher" nap, and it's only mid-afternoon.) Maybe the phone is about to ring. (No, it's still just sitting there.) Oh no! Oh my goodness! Unless you get really creative or worthless, *you're really going to have to write this paper!* And so, you're staring at a blank area of screen or paper where words should be appearing, but they aren't. You check the time again.

Scene two: You're staring at a screen or paper that's covered with writing. It's one of many. You're swamped with ideas; you've got too much material. You're ready to write the paper now, but *there's just too much stuff!* You just can't use it all. "Okay," you say, "I'll just have to pick the best bits, the ideas and facts that go together most effectively, and organize those into a first draft."

Which situation would you rather be in? No question: Like money, food, land, and many other things, too much is much better than too little. It's easier to prune a bush than create one. So, you're ready to write when you have too much to say, when you know you're going to have to cut some pretty good stuff just because you don't have the room or the need for it. The goal in this section is to think about how you can get to that point of plentitude.

The most important step toward writing from an abundance of ideas is to view your writing as a process, as an evolving piece of work. You simply cannot expect, unless you are a genius and also very lucky, to sit down, with no preparation, and produce a significant piece of writing by starting at the beginning and writing straight through to the end. Preparation is essential: You need knowledge and ideas to work with as you draft and revise. There are a few tricks that this section will share with you—invention strategies, they're usually called—which are useful for retrieving and organizing what you know, generating new connections and relationships, and even creating new ideas.

Invention strategies particularly draw attention to the notion that writing is a powerful tool not only for communicating knowledge, but also for creating it. In the last few decades, many people have rediscovered the insight that writing about something is an especially effective way of learning about it—of learning both what you know and (sometimes) what you need to find out.

Freewriting

Freewriting, the first invention strategy we'll consider, is a very popular way of generating ideas. With Peter Elbow's enthusiastic championing, freewriting has become a standard part of writing instruction around the world; it's very likely you've already had some practice freewriting. It is based on the realization that we often limit and even block our creativity by focusing on grammar, phrasing, logic, neatness, and all sorts of minute particulars. In ancient times, classical rhetoricians made invention a separate stage of composing, distinct from arrangement and style, because they perceived how logic and style can interfere with spontaneous creativity.

To engage in freewriting, of course, you simply focus your attention on your subject (if you have one) and write as fast as you can, without censoring, without rephrasing, without editing, without evaluating. Just put your mind in gear and let it go—wide open—for a set period of time. Ten minutes per freewriting is a good idea, for most people; you may want to try some longer and shorter sessions to see what suits you best.

This sounds ridiculously easy, and it often is. But you may find your attention wandering from your subject, in which case you shouldn't be frustrated; just focus again on the topic. If you find yourself with nothing to say, simply say something dumb, anything, or write "I have nothing to say; don't know what to say, nothing comes to mind," until something does come to mind. You can even speculate on why you have nothing to say. The important thing is to keep the pen moving.

Imagine that you've been given this assignment: "In a letter to your local newspaper, express your opinion on the appropriateness of media investigations into the private lives of presidential candidates." Here is an example of freewriting on that topic:

> Is a politician's private life really private? Is this a dumb question? Don't the basic rights and privileges of our country apply to all its citizens, including politicians? So private life has to be private, right? On the other hand, politicians are (or aspire to be) *public* servants, don't they? In offering to be our leaders, don't politicians, in effect, expose themselves to our scrutiny?
>
> I don't know. I'm hungry: Both sides of this issue seem plausible to me. It's a stupid question. I don't care, do I? It is kind of interesting to see what scandalous things the media can turn up. Real-life soap opera. I guess I should be embarrassed to find someone's troubles entertaining. Maybe I just don't see politicians as real people. They're just actors on a stage? But, of course, they are real people, and they can have a real impact on everybody's life, including my own. I should take this seriously, I guess.
>
> But how can it be decided? I think the public has the right to know, and I think the politician has the right to privacy. Something's gotta give here.
>
> How to get beyond this dilemma? How? I don't know. I can't think of anything. Maybe we could ask which of these valid concerns has more weight? Which gorilla is bigger? One could argue that if one person's rights are violated, then the whole system is called into question. But that really isn't true, is it? Individuals' rights have been violated in the past, and the system is still in place. On the other hand, should a

truly evil person attain a position of power, our system might possibly be in jeopardy. At the least, harm could be done that is more serious than the violation of privacy.

Hey! I think I've figured out what position I want to take: I would like to know everything about a politician's character, including anything in his or her private life that might conceivably affect on-the-job performance. Anyone who offers to run should, in my view, realize they surrender some of their privacy. We may lose some good candidates this way, but with 260 million people, surely there are some good people with nothing to hide.

Looping

Looping involves returning to material already written and focusing on some part of it in another session of writing. As you read over your freewriting or your draft, you'll probably find that some ideas seem useful, others don't. Circle those words, phrases, sentences, or paragraphs that seem to be heading in the right direction and ignore the rest. Then use the circled materials as the basis for further freewriting and drafting. If you're working at a computer, simply block off the parts you like and lift them out of the text. Move them into another file that will continue to evolve into your essay.

It's always possible that as you loop back over your materials, you won't find *anything* you like. Don't be discouraged, and don't crumple the paper and practice your Michael Jordan imitation; just write some more. You may find, as you go along, that these rejected materials actually contain something valuable. And it's also always possible, in theory anyway, that in looping you'll find your draft is just about perfect. People do, occasionally, hit a hole-in-one.

If you have trouble deciding which materials to keep as you're looping, here's a tip: If you've written something that surprised you, that you really didn't expect to say when you began writing, then that material is probably good. Loop on it and see what happens.

Here's an example of looping:

Assignment

Imagine that the Board of Trustees at your school is beginning to consider whether to begin a football program. They have asked for student input in this process, and you have been selected as the student representative. Write the brief statement you will make to the Board.

Freewriting

Money is an important consideration. It will cost money to start a program, although in the long run the program may make money. There is, however, no guarantee that football will generate money any time soon. We could look at other places and see how much it costs to start a football program. Why would the Board be interested in starting football anyway? Was its interest financial? Are any actions not financially motivated in the final analysis? Yes, sometimes people do things for altruistic motives. What would those be for football? Prestige for the school? School spirit?

Looping

Perhaps as the student representative, I should point out to the Board that the short-term financial aspects would appear to be negative. I think students would be most concerned that football might take money away from other programs, or even raise the tuition. Although a football program might eventually make money, in the short run it would cost money. Here's my position: I believe students would support the idea if the Board can use funds that would not affect tuition or education.

Cubing

Cubing is a kind of directed freewriting that lets you quickly explore a topic from six different perspectives (a cube has six sides—hence the name): describing, comparing, associating, applying, tracing, and evaluating. Each of these perspectives, which will all be explained in a moment, brings different questions into play. Focus on the questions raised by each perspective and freewrite for three to five minutes in response to those questions. After going through all six sides, which should take only about half an hour, you should have a good bit of material to work with.

Here are the questions followed by a brief example.

1. *Describe.* What are the features of the subject? What are its parts? What is its appearance? Form? Color? Thickness?

To engage these questions, one obviously must view the subject as a static thing, which is in some cases odd but nevertheless often illuminating. Let's say, in thinking about the project discussed in the looping section (speaking to a Board of Trustees about starting football), I decide to try cubing to see if I can get some deeper insight into football.

> Football can be divided into the team and the fans. If we
> think of it as an object, through much of the week football
> is a fairly small entity, involving a hundred or so people
> at any school. On Saturdays, however, football swells
> quickly for a few hours to involve thousands of people.
> And throughout the week, thousands not directly involved
> will discuss the team. So, football as an entity is more than
> coaches and players; it extends itself throughout the
> community.

2. *Compare.* How does the subject compare to other subjects? What is it like? What is it not like? What does it have in common with other subjects?

Football seems most like soccer. You have a ball and two teams and two goals. Soccer is more important internationally, but football has just about displaced baseball as the American sport. Football is, in my opinion, much more exciting than soccer, requiring more teamwork and precise timing and more set plays and strategies. To be sure, the action is just about continuous in soccer, but the scoring is usually low. Football is certainly more violent. Soccer is often a rough sport, admittedly, and the players don't wear pads. Football involves many collisions every play: the object of the game at any given moment for one side is to knock a player on the other side to the ground. In fact, football is so violent and brutal, one might wonder if it's really healthy, psychologically or physically. Yet, many people I consider to be very kind and intelligent love the sport. I wonder if my audience will have considered this negative side? Should I bring it up?

3. *Associate.* What do you associate with this subject? Letting your mind wander, what can you connect to this subject? What unexpected, creative links can you make between this subject and something else?

Football—I associate it with tailgating, and with parties, and with getting dressed up. A football team would probably stimulate takeout food sales and clothing sales in the fall. Perhaps those merchants would like to help support football?

Being more creative, I could associate football games and religious worship: crowds of people come together once a week to sit as a group, raise their voices, stand up at intervals, and then go home. But football seems sometimes to be taken more seriously? More passionately anyway? Do people contribute more or less time and money to football? Is it more or less satisfying?

4. *Trace.* Can you trace the progress of the subject? How did it begin? How did it develop? What will it become?

> I don't know much about the history of football. I should do some research perhaps on that. Fifty years or so ago, I would guess, football players wore helmets that were just leather caps. I've seen pictures. The players looked scrawny and underfed. Today they wear high-impact, lightweight plastic polymers (this sounds good; check whether it's at all accurate) with extensive padding; the face masks for some players look like cages, and some even have plexiglas shields to protect their faces entirely.
>
> Probably every piece of equipment has been improved to allow stronger, faster, heavier players to crash into each other with incredible force without killing each other on impact. But the pads have not evolved enough to protect the players entirely, for in any given game injuries seem to abound. Are these injuries worth it? Is football really any more dangerous than basketball or volleyball or soccer? I'll have to research that.

5. *Apply.* What applications does the subject have? What is its use? What problems can it be used to solve?

> Football can be used to raise money. It can increase school spirit. It can teach lessons about team work and dedication and effort. Football can also stimulate a local economy; construction, restaurant, and lodging businesses may all benefit. Football may also provide an outlet for aggression, both for participants and spectators. It may encourage some students to continue their education in order to play.

6. *Evaluate.* Is the subject good? Is it bad? What can be said in its favor? What can be said against it? How does its present state compare to its ideal?

Football can be a positive force, contributing to personal growth and stimulating economic growth for a school and a community. Football can also cause serious, sometimes even fatal, injury to participants, even at the high school levels and below. Football can promote physical fitness, to be sure. And most injuries are not serious. Like any sport, football can distract its participants from other (more important) activities.

As you can see, this cubing exercise produced many ideas and some avenues for research. Word processing tip: Create a file containing all the cubing questions. Then, anytime you begin to invent ideas, you can insert this file of questions into your draft file, using them as a series of writing prompts to produce potential material.

Brainstorming, Collaborating, Clustering

Brainstorming is another activity designed to help writers explore a topic quickly. It can be used by one person or a group, and it seems to have become particularly popular with business executives, perhaps because it allows a group of people to share ideas in a nonjudgmental, nonthreatening way. When a group of people brainstorm, there is often a synergistic effect as the participants draw inspiration from each other.

Brainstorming is like freewriting: There are no wrong suggestions; anything you want to say is fine. But, instead of freely writing in sentences, in brainstorming you can use single words or phrases. The ideas suggested can be listed, or they can be written down as a network, with lines drawn to show connections. Just set a brief time limit (say 10–15 minutes) and throw out ideas, writing them all down without censoring or judging. There's no telling what will turn out to be useful.

Consider this task:

    Although your parents can readily afford to send you to college, they believe that it would be a good idea for you to get a part-time job while you are in college. They both worked their ways through college, paying all their own expenses. They believe the discipline they learned then was as important as the college courses. They feel that you have it much easier than they did and you shouldn't complain about a little part-time job.

    You disagree. Your job is to think up reasons why you should be allowed to devote yourself fully to college study and why you should not have to take a part-time job.

Figure 2.3 is a sample brainstorming operation devoted to that task.

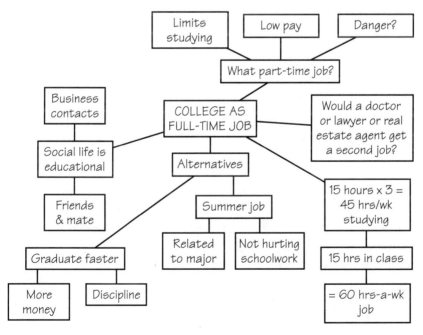

✦ **Figure 2.3**   Brainstorming Example

After lots of ideas are out on the table, clustering is the act of grouping related items together. Although the items may already be related to some extent by the brainstorming activity itself, clustering looks for additional or different connections. For instance, the items generated by the part-time job brainstorming could be regrouped into financial considerations and academic considerations. With this regrouping, a more organized and, therefore, more persuasive presentation of the argument is already starting to emerge. Compare a part-time job during the school year to a full-time job in the summer, and you will see clearly that the summer job will produce as much, if not more, money and a better academic career.

As more and more people are networked on-line, collaborative efforts of all sorts, including brainstorming, are bound to become more common. Collaborative assignments in classrooms are also increasingly common. While most writers enjoy having someone to bounce ideas around with, a caution needs to be noted: namely, your sources still need to be acknowledged, even when those sources include a group working together. If the resulting document is signed by all the participants, then there's no problem; but if the document is signed by an individual, or by part of a collaborative group, then the collaboration needs to be acknowledged. One could argue that the people who participate freely in a collaboration are tossing their ideas out for everyone's use, but it is nonetheless appropriate for you to do your best to give credit where credit is due. (Chapter 6 provides detailed information about when and how to document sources.)

In collaborative brainstorming, it's especially important to suppress any negative or critical reactions. Participants need to feel completely secure, able to say whatever occurs to them. Creating such an inviting environment in a collaboration is not always easy, but following a few simple rules will help any aspect of a collaborative writing process go more smoothly.

✦ *Tips for Collaborative Writing*

- To make the best use of the various talents in any group, the members need to find out what those talents are. Therefore, some time should be invested at the beginning of a collaborative project to get to know each other; at the least, each member should talk specifically about how he or she might contribute to the task at hand. This discussion could be linked to some consideration of just what individual jobs need to be performed in order to carry out the entire task.

- If someone in the group offers an idea that seems dumb, then ignore it, or try to find something useful in it. But if the group seems to be moving toward a consensus that seems wrong to you, don't hesitate to disagree. There would seem to be little point in collaborating if different opinions aren't going to be expressed and discussed. And brainstorming is likely to produce conflicting and even contradictory ideas.

- Take the advice of marriage counselors (collaborative writing is a little like a short-term, multi-partner marriage): avoid accusing statements that begin with "you," such as "You are not doing as much work as I am"; instead, try for open-ended statements that begin with "I," such as "I feel as if I'm being overwhelmed with this project; is there some way we can rethink everybody's assignments?"

- Don't assume that the writing will go faster simply because more people are involved. It may take more time, but one hopes the result will be worth it.

(continued)

> • Impose some structure on collaborative sessions, but not
> too much. Plan how much time you're going to spend on
> particular tasks, but then don't be obsessive about follow-
> ing your plan if progress is being made.

Asking Questions

Cubing is valuable because it offers a prescribed set of questions
you can rely on to generate material. Questions are vital to any
project; they are often more important and harder to find than answers. You are not, of course, limited to the questions presented in
cubing, and you will find it helpful to spend some time, if possible,
just thinking of questions related to any assignment. In a sense,
the art of thinking depends on the art of asking questions.

Don't worry about answers at this point. The idea is to free up
your creativity, to generate lines of inquiry. Therefore, you can
even pose questions that are (or seem to be) impossible to answer.
Or, you can come at a problem that is already solved from a different angle. Often, we stop with the first answer, when a better one
might emerge with more consideration. Shift your attention from
the obvious aspects and look elsewhere. You may have heard the
story of the truck that got stuck under an overpass: just as the engineers were going to blowtorch the top off the truck, a bystander
suggested letting the air out of the tires. Removing the truck top
(where the problem was) would have worked, but letting the air
out of the tires (seemingly, not where the problem was) was certainly much easier.

One of the most familiar sets of questions, employed by jour-
nalists, asks the following: Who? What? Where? When? Why?
How? Another well-known strategy of questioning involves dis-
placing your subject in space or time. Imagine the subject, for instance, in one hundred years: How will it have changed? How will

it be perceived? Or imagine the subject one hundred years before now? Or imagine the subject in another place or culture: How will it change? Or how will it be perceived?

You can also ask questions about the name of the subject: What is the history of its name? What words are associated with it? Has the name changed? Have the connotations changed?

You can elicit questions from your friends, asking them what they would like to know about the subject. Or you can imagine people from various backgrounds and conjure up the questions they would ask. You can, in fact, get questions from anywhere: The important thing is to collect them. Start a page or computer file of your favorite questions. Then, when you get ready to start inventing, you only have to think of answers!

Pro-and-Con Thinking

It is not uncommon in a discussion for one party to play "devil's advocate," as it is usually called. The purpose of such role playing (usually) is to help the parties explore more aspects of the subject than would likely emerge in a one-sided discussion. Having an opponent is a useful stimulus.

Our legal system is, in fact, based on the effectiveness of such an adversarial system. The prosecution tries to prove the accused guilty. The defense tries to show innocence. Neither side is asked to determine guilt or innocence ahead of time; their jobs are, instead, to make the best case for their respective sides.

Pro-and-con thinking as an invention strategy can been envisioned as a conversation with a devil's advocate or as a trial with opposing lawyers. You explore your topic by offering first one view and then its opposition. You don't have to limit your conversation to only two voices, but you are likely to find it helpful to keep two antithetical views prominent.

Some writers have considerable trouble with this invention strategy, which forces them to make arguments they don't really believe in. Just keep in mind that you are making a hypothetical case. No one will force you to endorse any position you maintain in a pro-and-con exercise. You shouldn't, in fact, assume that a lawyer who defends an accused murderer is in favor of murder. Instead, he is playing a role in a system of justice, which is designed to expose the truth by positioning the prosecution against the defense. Besides, if you do believe passionately in either the pro or the con, making the opposing case will help you to anticipate objections and counterarguments, making your own position ultimately stronger in the long run. Although in some kinds of writing endeavors you might not be concerned with what an audience will think, in many cases you are; if you aim to explain, or persuade, or analyze, or even entertain, then you'll need to think about what your audience already thinks and feels. Pro-and-con thinking exercises can be especially helpful in revealing the complexities of different possible positions.

Some topics are indeed so polarizing, so passionately held, that many teachers discourage students from writing about them on the assumption that many students will have difficulty being open-minded enough to discuss the topic intellectually and that most students will also have difficulty thinking of anything that hasn't already been said many times before. Abortion, for instance, is one of those often-forbidden topics. Yet, it is a very important issue, one that our culture continues to grapple with; it seems a shame to discourage its consideration. In the brief example below, I try to show how pro-and-con thinking can help you open up such a charged and oftentimes closed-off topic. The strategy here is simply for the writer to create two voices, one pro and one con, and let them argue it out, giving each side the strongest possible case, regardless of what the writer ultimately believes.

Example of Pro-and-Con Thinking

Speaker 1: Abortion is murder. We cannot possibly tolerate murder.

Speaker 2: How can you say it is murder? Is removing an appendix or a spleen murder?

Speaker 1: A baby is not an appendix. It is a person.

Speaker 2: A baby is a person, but a one-day-old fetus is not a baby or a person. A spleen can respond to stimulus and so can shrimp. A fetus may be alive in a sense, but it is not a human being.

Speaker 1: If a fetus is not a human being, then what is it? When a fetus is born prematurely, we do not discard it. We try to save it, and we often succeed.

Speaker 2: Okay, I grant you that if a fetus can survive, then it could be considered a baby. But until it can survive outside the mother, it is a part of the mother, and she can control its fate. In the first few weeks of life, a fetus is no more than an assemblage of cells; it is the potential for life, but not life. It is really no more aware or alive than an egg or a sperm alone. A gerbil is closer to being a person than such an early fetus.

Speaker 1: A one-year-old cannot survive on its own outside its mother. Is a one-year-old not a person? Should the mother control the one-year-old's fate? And a gerbil can never be a person. A fetus is a person, just a very tiny and immature one.

[This could be continued, of course.]

Journals, Commonplace Books

A *commonplace* is, of course, a wise or memorable saying, and a commonplace book is a notebook in which a writer collects quotations along with facts, figures, questions, and anything else that might be of future use. It's a great idea to set aside a special notebook and keep it handy, recording passages or phrases or facts that are especially striking or important.

You can also use your journal or commonplace book to list new words and to meditate on their meanings. You can summarize what you've learned in class lectures or discussion (a really effective way to enhance your learning). You can respond to reading assignments. You can record what's going on in your life and use the space to write about its meaning and significance. In a variety of ways, you can store up materials for future use. Virtually all writers have some kind of commonplace book to keep track of their ideas, a space to work things out on paper. You should too.

✦ *Invention Strategies*

- **Freewriting:** Write without stopping for ten minutes. Rest and repeat.

- **Looping:** Identify promising passages in your freewriting and write quickly developing those passages.

- **Cubing:** Describe, compare, associate, trace, apply, evaluate.

- **Brainstorming:** Throw out ideas without censoring them. Record the information and look for the connections.

- **Questions and Answers:** Generate questions; try to answer them.

- **Pro-and-Con Thinking:** Construct a conversation enacting opposing sides of a subject.

- **Commonplace Book:** Write down useful or striking quotations or ideas.

3

Drafting

*Never forget that writing is as close as we get to keeping a
hold on the thousand and one things.*

—Salman Rushdie (1985)

✦ ✦ ✦

Your Purpose

This chapter talks about how you can get from a bunch of disorganized ideas, pushing and shoving in various directions, to a finished piece of coherent, effective, satisfying writing. The journey
can be arduous, and you may sometimes feel as if "you can't get
there from here." And indeed, you *can't* get there from anywhere
(or know when you've arrived) until you know where "there" is—
until you have a definite goal or purpose. Good writers believe that
they can figure out where they're going as they go along; and so
they jump in and start writing, even when they're not sure what
to say.

Sometimes, to be sure, there's no question where you have to go (Charleston, to be in a wedding), just as sometimes there is no question what your goal in writing will be (explain to the Charleston police why your parking ticket should be waived). In such cases, you do have some choices about actual details, but your main purpose is set. Other times, however, your destination and activities aren't that clear, and the purpose may well evolve as the process unfolds. In at least one way, writers are more fortunate than travelers; you can't go back and delete some part of a trip when you realize later that it really didn't fit in with your purpose. But in writing, as long as you're still drafting, you can make changes, both small and huge. The motion of drafting an essay moves forwards and backwards, as you constantly consider what to say next and reconsider what you've already said.

If purpose is crucial to writing, how do you find a purpose if one is not already assigned? By writing, of course. You engage in invention strategies, perhaps doing research and talking to other people, and you write and think about your topic until you have an idea that effectively focuses your effort. Drafting is the process of learning precisely what you want to say: as the British writer E. M. Forster put it in his often-quoted remark, "How can I know what I think until I see what I say?"

In expressive writing, your purpose is likely to be limited by the subject, if at all. If you're writing, say, a personal essay that describes a friend or tells a story, your expressive purpose is simply to describe or narrate or speculate as richly, fully, and revealingly as you choose. A more defined purpose emerges for, say, a description of that friend for a particular audience, or a lab report for a professor, or an explanation of how to work a washing machine for students who have never lived away from home before. Once readers enter the picture, the purpose has to take them into account. The goal then becomes to shape the description or narration for that audience, taking into account what they might already know and feel.

Since no human being has a completely objective vantage point on life, any effort to convey information involves some assumption and opinion. At the least, the writer has to decide what holds the information together: readers generally are frustrated by unconnected, unrelated data. So the writer who wants to explain a process or concept—or to describe a person, place, or thing—must make some decisions about how the information is related and unified. Readers want to know, in other words, "What is this about? What's the point?" Thus, even the writer who is attempting to convey information clearly and "objectively" needs to determine an organizing central idea.

Thus, all effective writing, including even poetry and personal expression, involves an element of persuasion. To put it another way: All coherent writing has what is usually called a "thesis," a controlling idea; and readers will naturally try to assign a thesis to any piece of writing. Even readers of incoherent scribblings will usually try to impose some sense on what they're reading, to make it add up to something. Even a phone book does more than simply convey information; it also attempts in various ways to persuade you that the phone company is organized, reliable, public-spirited, and trustworthy. Even the most purely personal expression is subjected to this basic expectation, even if the author is the only reader. We simply cannot avoid asking "What was the point of this?"—unless we conclude that the writing doesn't work—doesn't do anything—and that the writer actually didn't have anything to say.

What Is a Controlling Idea?

Since readers expect effective documents of all sorts to be organized by some controlling idea, let's consider for a moment what an effective purpose looks like. For starters, a thesis is necessarily a sentence. The purpose of an essay cannot be "taxes on the middle class." That is a subject. Here's a thesis: "We should increase [or lower, or flatten, or abolish, or something else] taxes on the middle class."

But a good thesis is more than just a sentence. Consider this one: "The middle class pays 85 percent of the taxes in the United States." That statement, it would seem, is either a fact or not. It would appear to be tough to organize an argument around this observation, although it might be a very important piece of support for some other assertion. I say it would be "tough" rather than "impossible," because under certain conditions, this statement could be considered arguable. Let's say economists who have studied the matter agree that the middle class pays 72 percent of the taxes. And let's say that you discover a flaw in this research, something that the other economists have overlooked, and by your calculations the middle class actually pays 85 percent of the taxes. In that situation, the statement that "the middle class pays 85 percent of the taxes in the United States" actually becomes a powerful controlling purpose. It should probably be restated as a thesis, however, to reflect its rhetorical situation: "Although economists have agreed that the middle class pays 72 percent of the taxes, my research shows the figure actually should be 85 percent."

If you were asked to write a report that explained the proportion of taxes paid by the middle class, then your controlling idea could be a simple declaration of that percentage: everything in your report would then be orchestrated to make that central statement detailed and clear. You might want to define "middle class," explain what you mean by "taxes" (federal, state, or local? income or sales?), and show exactly how the 85 percent figure breaks down. Thus, what would be a perfectly acceptable controlling idea for an informational report ("the middle class pays 85 percent"), would be an unpromising thesis for an argument.

Here's another example:

The most effective tax increase would target the middle class because they pay 85 percent of the taxes.

Is this a good controlling idea? At first glance, this assertion might seem so obvious that one could hardly argue about it. It could not structure an informational essay, however, because it is not a matter of fact. You would have to persuade an audience to agree with this statement by defining "effective": effective in what sense? While the middle class already pays most of the taxes, and might, therefore, appear to be the logical place to raise taxes, one could argue that more taxes on the middle class would harm the economy by reducing the spending power of those who purchase most of the goods and services. Or, one could argue that more taxes on the middle class will actually enlarge the middle class, by redistributing more money to people who are currently considered to be in the lower class. Or, one could argue that raising middle-class taxes will reduce tax revenues by discouraging earning and spending. Or, one could argue that "effective" is the wrong evaluator. Or, any number of other things. The statement thus seems to have some good potential as a thesis: It is arguable.

Thus, we've arrived at this understanding: Informational writing should have a controlling sentence, a central fact or observation that organizes everything else. For persuasive writing, the controlling idea should be a thesis, an arguable sentence. Just to make sure you understand this crucial point, let's evaluate by way of review a few more controlling ideas:

1. Genetic engineering will be an important part of medicine in the future.

    > To control an *informational* essay, this idea would need to be made more specific, stating precisely how genetic engineering will be important. For an *argument*, this statement might not be very promising: most scientists would readily accept it. For some audiences, however, who might believe that genetic engineering is dangerous or unnatural or even evil, this assertion could structure a lively argument.

2. Litchfield Beach is on an extraordinarily beautiful stretch of the South Carolina coast.

> An acceptable controlling idea for an informational essay, if it is made specific. It's probably not a good thesis; anyone who's been there would say it is a fact. One could argue, I suppose, that it is not "extraordinarily beautiful" since that is a matter of taste, but as a thesis for an argument, it does not seem promising.

3. Satan is the real hero of *Paradise Lost*.

> Not really suitable for an informational essay because it would have to be argued; it's not a question of fact. Thus, it's an engaging thesis, unexpected and controversial. It has, however, already been argued by William Empson and refuted by, among others, Shelby Foote; so you would need some new angle to avoid repeating what's already been said. And you would want to acknowledge the prior arguments, if you knew anything about them.

4. I like Ross Perot.

> It is difficult to say whether this assertion would make a good argument or not. If the essay supports the writer's affection for Perot in a persuasive way, then the real thesis is something like "Ross Perot was a good candidate," or "You should admire Ross Perot as I do." If the essay merely asserts that the writer likes Perot, it would be very difficult to argue. How can anyone else say the writer doesn't like Perot?

5. As a presidential candidate, Ross Perot never had a chance.

> Could be a good thesis: it seems controversial and arguable. It might also be a good controlling idea for an

informational essay, discussing polling data and political analysis that reveals Perot's weakness.

6. The worldwide decline in many frog species signals the eventual doom of the planet.

> A striking thesis, if it can be plausibly supported. It probably claims too much, however, thereby weakening its own force. Rather than saying the whole planet is "doomed," which would be difficult, if not impossible, to argue convincingly, it would be more plausible and thereby effective to argue only that the missing frogs suggest we may be in some serious ecological danger.

Does It Have to Be Narrow?

Most textbooks will tell you that a thesis should be narrowed down. For instance, if you begin with the topic "trees," the conventional wisdom says you should limit your discussion in the following fashion:

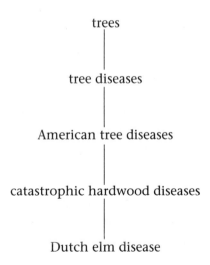

trees

tree diseases

American tree diseases

catastrophic hardwood diseases

Dutch elm disease

The logic behind this narrowing advice is that you shouldn't take on a large, general, or abstract topic; you should limit your essays to topics you can handle: small, specific, concrete. Instead of an essay on the problem of evil, you should write on sudden infant death syndrome, narrowing down the topic like this:

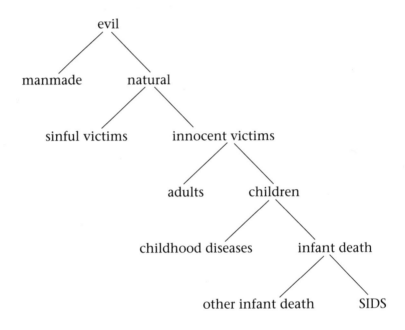

The problem with this conventional wisdom is that it tends to prevent anyone from thinking about large and complex issues. It might be difficult to write an essay on trees or on the problem of evil, but such essays might also be extremely valuable. Admittedly, you couldn't cover everything about trees in a three-page essay, but you couldn't cover everything we know about Dutch elm disease either. The key to a successful essay, in fact, is not whether your controlling idea is large or small, or whether you say everything that could possibly be said about it, but rather whether your writing is focused, interesting, and compelling: is your audience satisfied? If you really wanted to argue that "trees are the most valuable plants on earth" or that "trees are capable of emotional response," I'd hate to see you settle instead for a history of Dutch elm disease.

At this point, you should have some idea of what a controlling purpose is, and how a particular writing situation really affects whether a statement will work well or not as a controlling idea for an informational or persuasive work. The writer's purpose is shaped not only by what the writer wants to do, but also by what the audience already knows and believes. In the next section, let's look more closely at how considerations of the reader affect the writer's purpose and everything else.

Your Reader

Three Conditions

The purpose of an argument (almost always, anyway) is, of course, to persuade the audience to agree with the thesis; this goal should determine where the thesis appears. Often a thesis is explicitly stated near the beginning of an argument, but a thesis can actually appear anywhere in an essay, and it can even not appear at all—being implied. If the audience will automatically oppose the main point—or be at the outset unable to understand it—then it makes sense to hold the thesis until later when a foundation for accepting or understanding it has been built. If the audience will be strongly opposed to the thesis, no matter how it is introduced or supported, then the best strategy may be to leave it unstated, allowing the audience to come to that conclusion on their own.

Such strategic considerations regarding the placement of your thesis are prudent even if the piece of writing is not viewed as an argument in the strictest sense. If you've been hired by the Tobacco Institute to do an overview of research on second-hand smoke and you genuinely want them to grasp the facts in as unbiased and thorough a manner as possible, then you probably don't want to say at the beginning, "The research clearly shows that second-hand smoke is dangerous; the risk of cancer for passive smokers is about a thousand times greater than the one-in-a-million lifetime cancer risk considered acceptable for other environmental contaminants" (*Consumer Reports*, January 1995, 32–33). To convey this information to that audience, you will likely need to explain in some detail, step by step, what the research shows and lead up to this conclusion at the end. Conveying information, as I've noted, always involves some element of audience analysis and persuasion, and in some situations that element is large.

To make sure you understand the relationship between the audience and the controlling idea, let's look at three conditions that should be satisfied:

1. *The controlling idea should be news.* If your audience will accept your main point as common knowledge, unremarkable and obvious, then why should they read you? Your writing will not be conveying information or arguing a contestable point. The make-up of the audience in this regard is crucial: It would seem entirely unnecessary to inform anyone, for instance, that the earth circles the sun—unless your audience consisted of primitive tribesmen, the Flat Earth Society, or thirteenth-century Italian Popes, in which case you do have an argument. Even a statement of fact such as "The Nazi Holocaust killed six million Jews" can become, for some (loony-bin) audiences, an arguable point; for other audiences (high school history students, for instance), this assertion may well be information. Although these are extreme examples, they do reinforce this commonsense point: Think carefully about what your audience will consider arguable and informational. It should be surprising; it should be "news."

2. *The controlling idea should also be presented in terms that the audience can understand.* I have explained the argument of my book on Samuel Johnson to eighteenth-century scholars, to my students, and to my family. My thesis didn't change, but the wording for these three audiences was dramatically different, as you might imagine. To understand your main point, the audience

may require not only that individual terms be explained, but also that the entire background or context be revealed.

How can you know what a particular audience will understand? (For that matter, how can you know what an audience will consider to be news?) The easiest way to know, obviously, would be to ask them; if that's not possible, ask a sample of them. If that's not possible, you will just have to use your own good sense. Keep in mind, as you consider what the audience needs to know, that readers much more often complain that something doesn't make sense than they say, "That's just too clear."

3. *The controlling idea should be supportable and supported.* In this case, the audience helps determine what will count as support. If your explanation or argument depends on support from the Koran, for instance, and your audience is the Southern Baptist Convention, you really do not have a viable thesis because the Koran, for that audience, is not an authority. Any explanation you offer will likewise have to consider the audience's unfamiliarity and skepticism. So you will have to find another way of articulating your main point, a way that your audience can endorse.

Peer Editing

Since the audience so importantly determines the shape and content of any piece of writing, feedback from readers is extremely valuable. In many writing classes, students read each others' work and provide suggestions and appreciations—"peer editing," it's often called. You need not, of course, wait for your teacher to arrange for you to have readers; it's a good idea to seek them out yourself. The great thing about peer editing is that a reader doesn't have to be a great writer in order to tell you, "I got confused at the end of the first paragraph," or "I really liked the description of the hat; could you do more stuff like that, especially near the end?" Any reader who is willing to give an honest and thoughtful response can be very helpful to you.

Do be certain, however, that it is okay with your teacher to have other people respond to your work; and, especially, be sure to give credit to your readers for particular and substantive suggestions they make. For instance, if your roommate suggests a logical connection that you had not seen, it would be appropriate to insert a footnote, like this:[1]

[1]I am indebted to Rhonda Blankenship for this insight.

If a reader simply says, "I'm confused here," then you don't need to acknowledge that help, although you certainly may. Let's say, however, that a reader says this: "I'm confused here; why don't you just use the phrase 'last-hope medicine' rather than trying to name all these different kinds of alternative healing philosophies?" If you decide to use that phrase, then you should acknowledge its source in a note or a parenthetical comment: "I am indebted to Jack Spratt for the term 'last-hope medicine,'" or "'Last-hope medicine' is Jack Spratt's term." If you are ever in doubt whether to give someone credit, either go ahead and do it, or ask your teacher (or editor or supervisor). It's better to err on the side of generosity rather than take credit for someone else's words.

Your Text

What else, besides the main idea, does the audience affect? Everything, of course. Consider for a moment the sizes and shapes of the paragraphs in a piece of writing.

Paragraphs, like people, come in all shapes and sizes. Although there is, to be sure, an average size for paragraphs, it would be wrong to suggest that all paragraphs should come close to that average. If you have read or been told that a paragraph should have, say, six to eight sentences, you should forget that advice as soon as you can. Some paragraphs are much longer, some much shorter than average. Good writers vary paragraph size for the same reasons they vary sentence length and structure: (1) to avoid monotony and (2) to shape the material in an effective way. A very short paragraph, like a very short sentence, can be striking. And a very brief paragraph stands out.

Like this one.

That's because paragraphing is another form of punctuating, allowing you to vary the rhythm of your prose and impose a form on your material. Wherever a new paragraph begins, the reader is being cued to consider the subsequent material as a new unit. The indentation of a paragraph is, thus, a kind of pause, encouraging the reader to collect the ideas in the preceding paragraph and begin to look for its relationship to the following paragraph. Good writers usually provide explicit cues to the nature of that relationship.

Although a paragraph marks the end of one unit of thought, there is no requirement that every paragraph have a topic sentence stating its main idea. In fact, in a random sample of paragraphs from all sorts of texts, Richard Braddock found that less than a fifth contained topic sentences (*Research in Written Composition* [Champaign, Ill.: NCTE, 1963]). Why do so few paragraphs have topic sentences (even though students so often are told that every paragraph should have one)? For the most part, I suspect, because two or more paragraphs often function as a unit, unfolding an idea; and because sometimes topic sentences (like thesis sentences) are implied rather than expressed. If a paragraph has a topic sentence, it can appear anywhere: first, last, or in the middle. Your common sense, paying attention to the flow of your argument and the needs of your audience, will usually suggest the most effective placement.

If there are no hard and fast rules regarding the size of paragraphs, or the position of topic sentences, there is still one principle regarding the shape of paragraphs. Effective writers almost always use paragraphs that move from general to specific statements, from abstraction to detail, or vice versa. It is at least as important to vary your levels of generality and specificity as it is to vary the length and structure.

For instance, look at this paragraph:

> The union leaders are not being cooperative. The plant managers are being even less helpful. The whole mess seems headed for disaster. No viable solution has been offered.

Compare this paragraph, which offers just one level of generalization, to the one that follows, which alternates one level of generality with specific details:

> The union leaders are not being cooperative. They refuse to negotiate any of their demands. The plant managers are being even less cooperative; they will not even attend the joint meetings or talk to the union leaders. The whole mess seems headed for disaster: the plant will close or the union will be broken and some violence may break out. No viable solution has been offered, although some unworkable ideas, such as having the union purchase the plant or reducing the managers' pay to the level of the average workers' pay, have been put forth.

In almost any situation, the second paragraph would be considered better. It moves from general to specific. All abstractions or all details would be much less effective than a mixture.

If the size and shape of paragraphs depend on the audience, what about the shape of a text as a whole? Same thing, naturally. Let your purpose, your subject, and above all your audience guide the essay's form. Although virtually all college writing textbooks in recent years have advised against it, some students still come to college believing that good essays follow a certain prescribed format. In particular, a surprising number of students believe that an essay should begin with an opening paragraph that has the intellectual shape of an inverted pyramid, beginning with a broad generalization and narrowing down to a specific thesis. Then the model essay should have three paragraphs that support the thesis, each paragraph beginning with a thesis sentence. And then an essay should conclude with another pyramid, this one right-side up, beginning with a specific point, then developing a broad concluding statement, opening up the implications of the essay.

There are lots of problems with this advice. For one thing, it is almost impossible to find published essays that follow such a form. This is an artificial formula, found almost exclusively in schoolroom writing. For another thing, this format almost inevitably produces an essay that seems awkward, unnatural, and ineffective. The essay seems formulaic, like an exercise, and not like a real effort to say something to someone. Such a formula is perhaps okay in a few limited circumstances—you're writing under pressure in an exam, you've been instructed to follow the five-paragraph format. But most of the time you can do better.

To replace this tenacious writing formula, think about the form of an essay in other ways. First, think about the way a good piece of writing develops. Writing is not arranged so much according to paragraphing (which, we've noted, is a matter of punctuation), but by the kinds of logical structures discussed above: definition, description, narration, cause and effect, classification, and so forth.

Second, think in terms of any standard formats you'll need to follow. Lab reports, progress reports, scientific papers, and many other items have prescribed forms that are easy to figure out: just examine an example of the kind of thing you're trying to produce. An explanation of how to do something will naturally begin with an overview of the materials and the entire process, and then continue with a step-by-step description. Determining and then indicating what constitutes a step (deciding, in other words, how to divide up the process) is an important part of explaining an activity. Using headings or numbering the steps will help your readers understand what to do.

Finally, think in terms of an opening, a body, and a closing. As categories, these are admittedly very loose—but that is, in fact, a virtue. To the extent that anyone can offer advice for developing a piece of writing that would be applicable to every kind of writing, previous sections have already discussed strategies of development (see pages 27–42). Although there are likewise no universally successful formulas for opening or closing a piece of writing, there are generally applicable sample strategies. Keep in mind that these are only samples, not prescriptions. But if you understand the kinds of things writers do in order to open a particular essay, then you will be in a better position to invent an opening for your particular essay. (And remember, one of the best ways to learn what kinds of things writers do is to read widely and intently.)

Openers

We all know how crucial first impressions are in real life, and writing is about as real as life gets. We do sometimes get a chance to correct a bad first impression, but it is altogether possible your reader will turn away if the opening of your essay isn't promising. And even if your reader is obligated to read the rest of the essay, a poor beginning is likely to influence the perception of the rest of your essay. Obviously, you want to start well. But what is a good opener?

A good opener's most important quality, of course, is that it keeps the reader reading. But don't think that your opening therefore has to be cute or shocking or dramatic. You want to avoid any impression that your beginning is just a trick to keep readers reading. Instead, you want to give the impression that the essay is beginning quickly, providing important information immediately, and that the point of the essay will be worthwhile. Thus, you usually want to start fast, moving toward the point.

Of course, if you believe your audience will not be receptive to the point you want to make or will be unlikely to understand your point, then you want to move as quickly as possible to the information that will make your point understandable or acceptable. Just about the worst thing you can do, surely, is to offer some broad generalization or abstract observation that is slowly whittled down to a specific point.

Let's say, for instance, that you are being asked to write about a passage in George Eliot's often-taught novel, *Silas Marner*, a passage that compares the leisure of former days with those of the time in which Eliot is writing. Consider these two openings, both taken from actual papers:

Writer A

In *Silas Marner*, George Eliot distinguishes vividly between "old leisure" and "new leisure," applauding the former and condemning the latter.

Writer B

Literary writing has performed much in its history, providing amusement, education, and explanations of how the world has changed. George Eliot was one of the greatest writers of such literature. In this passage she accomplished all three of these, but her insight into how the world has changed is the most outstanding. She presented effectively her views of "old leisure" and "new leisure," and she depicts the literature of her time.

Writer B's opening is better only if the writer is being paid by the word or is attempting to solve the reader's insomnia. After four sentences, B still has not said anything useful about Eliot's comparison of the two kinds of leisure. We can see that writer B may be inching toward some kind of assertion; the paper began, after all, with the broadest of comments—"Literature has done many things in its time." But Writer A immediately says something specific about Eliot's treatment: old leisure is praised and the new leisure is condemned.

The opening sentence takes a stance, and we can easily imagine how the essay would develop in defense of this controlling idea. Notice also how Writer A quickly lets the reader know what the essay is about, naming the subject explicitly—Eliot and her novel, and the view of leisure it offers. I think any reasonable person would much rather read the rest of Writer A's work instead of Writer B's.

Starting quickly does require you to overcome the fear that you won't have enough to say. This is not a problem. If you spend time inventing, you'll generate enough material in your drafting stages that you will feel pressed to get it all in.

What other useful advice is there besides starting fast? You might try beginning with a quotation, if you can find one that is engaging and takes you to your starting point. Or, you can consider starting with a little story, an anecdote that illustrates where you want to begin. You can begin with an image, a picture. You can begin with a question. You might also try, occasionally, a dramatically brief sentence, one that makes a striking observation or claim. It's always possible to begin by defining the terms of your topic, but that approach has been used so often that it rarely seems fresh: most English teachers have read a huge stack of papers that begin by telling the reader how Webster defines this or that word, and they are tired of it.

✦ *Checklist for Openers*

- Does your audience need to be prepared to accept or understand your argument?

- If not, does your essay start fast?

- Does the essay provide necessary information as soon as possible, orienting the reader? If not, is there some strategic reason why?

- Does the essay give the impression of moving immediately toward an engaging point?

- Does the essay's opening employ an anecdote, or image, or question, or quotation, or some other drawing-in device?

Closers

First impressions are important, but the ending of a piece of writing is at least as important as any other part. You can engage the reader's attention and pursue an intelligent and convincing thesis, but this success is for nothing if the conclusion derails all your effort. Imagine a movie that draws you in at first, thrills and fascinates you in the middle, but then ends in a dumb and entirely unconvincing way. In some ways, we're even more disappointed than if the whole thing had been lousy.

But what constitutes an effective ending? What should you try to do? Most importantly, an ending should offer the reader something new. This advice may run counter to what some traditional textbooks (and their adherents) say, but it is supported by what good writers actually do. Simply reviewing the points you've already made isn't effective in a closing, especially if the essay is relatively brief: it's as if you're saying to the reader, "I really think you're too dumb to remember what I've just said, so I'm going to say it again." This "something new" in your conclusion can be some logical extension of your argument: for instance, in a scientific paper on the significance of Herpes Zoster (a particular kind of Herpes) as a marker for internal malignancy, Jeffrey Smith and Neil Fenske survey all the research related to this question and then end with a paragraph that draws a conclusion from the foregoing information:

> We agree that not all patients with HZ [Herpes Zoster] should be subjected to a malignancy workup. This would be an unnecessary and costly undertaking, not likely to be welcomed in today's climate of cost containment. But neither should a cavalier attitude be taken toward patients with HZ. Cases continue to occur (although rarely) in which HZ precedes a serious condition. Our recommendations are that all patients with HZ have a baseline history and physical examination. A further directed workup may be indicated on the basis of abnormal findings.
>
> —*Southern Medical Journal* 88:11 [November 1995] 1091

Thus, in their closing Smith and Fenske do not trace back over the ground they've already covered; they move forward to the point they have been working toward: not all patients with HZ need a malignancy workup, unless other indications emerge.

Other strategies for adding something new in your ending abound: for instance, argue for further study of the topic; apply the point you've already made; move to a larger context, drawing some generalization from your particular point; move to a smaller context, drawing some specific point from your general discussion. In any event, don't just review your points in the ending, unless the piece of writing has been lengthy and complex, and such a review would be valuable for the average reader. In that case, you're ending with a summary.

You do not, of course, want to claim too much in your conclusion or make grandiose applications that do not seem warranted by what has gone before. Be just as reasonable at the end as you have been (we hope) throughout. You probably do not want to say, "In view of such waste in the Social Security system, we ought simply to shut the entire government down." But you might want to say, "In view of such waste in the Social Security system, we ought not only to reform it but also to examine carefully every other governmental activity."

Let's look for a moment at another example, the last paragraph from Barbara Ehrenreich's essay in *Time* magazine, September 7, 1992, "Why the Religious Right is Wrong." The essay has been involved in doing two things: on the one hand, showing how Bush and the Republicans have been incorporating religion and religious appeals to "Judeo-Christian values" into their campaign; and, on the other hand, how the Founding Fathers emphatically intended for religion and government to be kept separate. Here's the closing paragraph:

> Over the years, there have been repeated efforts to invest the U.S. government with the cachet of divine authority. "In God We

Trust" was first stamped on currency in the 1860s. "Under God" was inserted into the Pledge of Allegiance during the McCarthyist 1950s. George Bush campaigned in 1988 to have the flag treated like a sacred object. And perhaps every revolution is doomed to be betrayed, sooner or later, by its progeny. It only adds insult to injury, though, when the betrayal is dressed up in the guise of "traditional values."

This closing paragraph, as you can see, expands the discussion by filling in some of the ground between the Founding Fathers and Bush. It suggests that the error the Republicans are currently making is not new: in between Bush and the Founding Fathers, who opposed state-approved religion (but also often referred, we might note, to a Supreme Being), other efforts apparently have been made to link state and church. The next-to-last sentence even suggests that linking church and state amounts to a betrayal of the country's founding principles, overturning the war for independence. And the final sentence adds a new point, leaving the reader with a strong assertion and the sense of an ending: the betrayal of the American tradition of separating religion and government is being presented as part of "traditional values," but it is, according to Ehrenreich, a betrayal of those values, overturning the "tradition." If one accepts Ehrenreich's starting point for the closer, that "In God We Trust" reflects a quest for Divine Authority (and not an expression of humble hope), then preparation for the final sentence has been ample. The final sentence clearly feels like the last sentence.

Conveying such a sense of closure is also important, although it's difficult to give advice about how to do it. When we are involved in a conversation, we usually have a good sense of when it is over. Occasionally one party will linger on, trying to extend the conversation when there really isn't anything more to say. One key to giving a sense of closure, of ending, is knowing when to quit. When you're finished, stop.

◆ *Checklist for Closers*

- Does the closing add something new? An extension, an application, a recommendation, a connection—some new idea based on the introduction and body?

- Does the closing give the reader a sense of closure? Is it clear that you have finished (and not just quit)?

- Have you avoided claims that are implausible or unwarranted?

4

Finishing

Interviewer: How much rewriting do you do?
Hemingway: It depends. I rewrote the ending of
Farewell to Arms, *the last page of it, thirty-nine times
before I was satisfied.*
Interviewer: Was there some technical problem there?
What was it that had stumped you?
Hemingway: Getting the words right.

—Paris Review Interview

Revising

For too many students, "revising" means simply "changing a few words, checking the spelling, and looking for typing errors." But for writers, including teachers of writing, revising means much more. "Revision" means "re-seeing," looking at anew—rethinking and rewriting. You may change a word, a phrase, a sentence; you may well find that whole sections need to be reworked, or deleted, or created.

Thus, the first step in revising is, in a sense, not a step at all but an attitude, taking for granted that your writing can be improved. You need to be willing to make changes, even large ones, even trying an entirely different approach. In the age of word processing, it is easy enough to make some back-up copies and then play with your draft. Indeed, there is in aggressive and effective revising a certain degree of playfulness; you have to be willing to try something else out, to fiddle, to start over.

Probably the worst attitude for revising is one of personal commitment to the way you said it the first time. It's always possible that the first draft is exactly perfect; but experienced writers will tell you that such a possibility rarely comes into being. It does not hurt to change your words. View it as a game, a puzzle, an opportunity to get something just right. That's the virtue of writing over speaking, isn't it? We get the chance to take it back and put it another way before the audience has even heard it. And if you don't like the changes, you can always put it back the way it was. Once you've assumed that your work can be changed and possibly improved, what should you do?

The Hard-to-Please Reader

Since most of us tend to have a certain affection for whatever we have managed to produce, there is a natural tendency to overlook problems and weaknesses, and to like whatever we see as we read over the current draft. Most readers, however, aside from your family and loved ones, are not necessarily so enamored of what you've written. Therefore, as your editing identifies words, sentences, passages, whatever to work on, you should *imagine a hard-to-please reader*, one who doubts whatever you say unless it's obvious or nailed down, who is impatient for you to get to your point, who picks nits at every opportunity. Imagine you are rewriting your draft *for that reader*, who is challenging your text in every way possible. Try to pull that tough reader in by acknowledging and anticipating alternative points of view, by tightening and brightening your prose, by eliminating distractions of any sort, including grammatical slip-ups (more on this in Chapter 5). Especially look for assertions that might be controversial or ambiguous without more support or elaboration. What is quite clear to you may be very confusing to a reader.

How about an example? Let's see what happens when we start to rewrite a passage with our hard-to-please (or htp) reader in mind. Here is the first paragraph from a student essay titled "Where Did Man Really Come From?":

> Ever since the beginning of modern times, people have always wondered about the origin of humankind. For some, this question of ancestry is a large puzzle with many missing pieces. For others, the solution does not seem unreachable. In fact, many feel that it is just a matter of time before man's origins are completely revealed. Among these optimistic people are anthropologists, archaeologists, and many other scientists. Though anthropologists only have various clues and guesses to work with today, they do have enough evidence to give a rather clear picture of man's history and development. Whether this evidence leads to the discovery of man's origins in the future is still to be seen.

Through the eyes of its creator, or similarly uncritical sight, this paragraph may seem fine. It's okay. But what would our hard-to-please (htp) reader say about it? Let's take it sentence by sentence. As we move along, pay close attention to both the attitude and the strategies being employed in revising.

> (1) Ever since the beginning of modern times, people have always wondered about the origin of humankind.

Does this first sentence seem somehow familiar? Our htp reader has seen lots of essays that make some huge claim like this one, and the htp reader usually wonders if the writer really knows what he or she is talking about. "Always" is one of those exhaustive terms, like "never," "completely," "entirely," "totally," "continuously," and others, that are sometimes used imprecisely, when the category really isn't exhaustive. Our htp reader would likely ask, "Do you really mean to say that human beings have devoted themselves solely to wondering about their origin, or that all of their wondering at least has been so focused? I doubt it."

You've got to admit: "often" would be better than "always." Similarly imprecise is "Ever since the beginning of modern times." What does that mean? "Quick," the htp reader says, "tell me exactly when did 'modern times' begin?" With television? The automobile? The steam engine? The rise of science? The recovery of classical civilization? Or classical civilization itself? Or maybe Egyptian civilization? With the discovery of fire? We have a span of many, many centuries here, and no way really to say within a few thousand years or so what the writer means.

Obviously, the sentence should be edited, perhaps to say precisely when modern times began and people started wondering; but I suspect that the writer really means something like "I don't know when people started wondering about this, but I bet it was a good while ago." If that's the case, and the writer doesn't know, then maybe it would be better just to move on to the topic: "People have often wondered about the origin of humankind."

I fear that this sentence, however, still would not engage our htp reader, who would find this opening obvious: "Of course they have; it goes without saying. What's your point?" Remembering the advice about openings offered above, the writer might well want to avoid this gesture toward a sweeping generalization at the outset, delete the first sentence, and move instead swiftly toward the topic. Do the next two sentences head that way?

(2) For some, this question of ancestry is a large puzzle with many missing pieces. (3) For others, the solution does not seem unreachable.

These sentences do seem to be heading somewhere. Sentence 2 sets up one category for whom the origin of humanity is a puzzle with missing pieces, and Sentence 3 sets up another category for whom "the solution" is reachable. The htp reader, looking carefully, might wonder about these two categories: the writer says, "For some" and "For others," but are they really separate? Don't the people who think that a solution is reachable also necessarily believe that there is a large puzzle with many missing pieces to begin with? If they don't believe there is a puzzle, how can they think there may be a solution? The two categories of people, actually, would appear to be "those who think we can solve the question of man's origin" and "those who think we cannot," since it is presumably a large puzzle for anyone. Thus far, one could argue, the paper really has said only this much:

> Some people believe the question of mankind's origin, a large puzzle with many missing pieces, can be solved.

In deleting the first sentence, we have lost the idea that this question has been around for some time (the writer isn't sure how long; maybe no one is), and so "the question of mankind's origin" might be altered to "the ancient question of mankind's origin." Also, an htp reader might worry over having a question "solved": questions are answered. The word "solved" really applies better to the puzzle, but the grammatical subject of "solved" is "question." Can this little problem be answered—I mean, solved? Certainly: simply change "question" to "problem":

> Some people believe the ancient problem of mankind's origin, a large puzzle with many missing pieces, can be solved.

What will our htp reader have to say about the next two sentences?

(4) In fact, many feel that it is just a matter of time before man's origins are completely revealed. (5) Among these optimistic people are anthropologists, archaeologists, and many other scientists.

What does Sentence 4 do for the reader, htp or otherwise? If we already know that some people believe the problem can be solved, don't we also already know that it is "just a matter of time" before that happens? Sentence 4 does shift from "some" to "many," which raises the question of what the writer really wants to say: what, in fact, is meant by "some" and "many"? Are these vague simply because the writer doesn't know, or do they actually refer to something meaningful?

Sentence 5 suggests that the writer really does have something fairly specific in mind, including "anthropologists, archaeologists, and many other scientists." Since Sentence 4 doesn't provide additional information, it can be deleted. Here then is what we have so far:

Some people believe the ancient problem of mankind's origin, a large puzzle with many missing pieces, can be solved. Among these optimistic people are anthropologists, archaeologists, and many other scientists.

Since Sentence 5 essentially explains who "some people are," the writer might consider combining these two sentences, like this:

Some people, including anthropologists, archaeologists, and many other scientists, believe the ancient problem of mankind's origin, a large puzzle with many missing pieces, can be solved.

On the other hand, this revision loses the reference to "these optimistic people," a characterization the writer might want to keep, depending on the rest of the paper.

Continuing:

(6) Though anthropologists only have various clues and
guesses to work with today, they do have enough evidence
to give a rather clear picture of man's history and development.

Even our htp reader would have to say that this sentence conveys
important information. Is there anything at all that isn't entirely
clear about it? Perhaps the htp reader might wonder exactly what is
meant by "clues and guesses." Unless you've studied anthropology,
you might have no idea what is meant here.

There is also something slightly worrisome about what each
part of the sentence says: the first part says anthropologists have
only "various clues and guesses to work with today," but the second part says they can "give a rather clear picture of man's history
and development." The htp reader may well wonder if the writer,
by pointing to the "various clues and guesses" (which seem slight),
intends to undermine the anthropologists' "rather clear picture" of
mankind's story. Can we draw a rather clear picture of all human
history from "various clues and guesses"? Does the writer mean to
be ironic?

To decide, we need to know what Sentence 6 is supposed to
accomplish. It stands between the statement that some scientists
believe the problem of humanity's origin can be solved, and this
statement:

(7) Whether this evidence leads to the discovery of man's
origins in the future is still to be seen.

Examined in context, the connecting role of Sentence 6 seems
clear: some scientists believe the origin can be found; they have already explained the history and development (this is Sentence 6);
but it still isn't clear if an understanding of the history and development will lead to an understanding of the origin.

Now that we understand the function of Sentence 6, the htp reader may wonder if it can be improved. Is everything clear? Can the reader say precisely what is being referred to? What, for instance, are the "clues and guesses"? Although readers with anthropological training probably have a good idea what these clues and guesses are, the rest of us probably don't. Are they related to the "large puzzle with many missing pieces"? Yes, upon consideration, it seems clear that the anthropologists are observing clues from and making guesses about the large puzzle with missing pieces. How might the writer help the reader to make this identification? The connecting role of Sentence 6 could be made more explicit by continuing the puzzle comparison from the previous sentence and by inserting the word "already" to highlight the progress made toward solving the problem mentioned in the first sentence. Here's how the revised passage looks so far:

> Some people, including anthropologists, archaeologists, and many other scientists, believe the ancient problem of mankind's origin, a large puzzle with many missing pieces, can be solved. Though anthropologists only have bits and pieces of the whole picture today, they already can describe rather clearly man's history and development. Whether this evidence leads to the discovery of man's origins in the future is still to be seen.

In the last sentence, Sentence 7, the phrasing of "the discovery of man's origins in the future" is worth noting because it is paradoxical: origins in the future? Does the phrase actually work, or is it just interesting but ultimately distracting? If it is determined to be distracting, "in the future" can easily enough be moved, like this: "Whether this evidence will lead in the future to the discovery of man's origins is still to be seen."
But the sentence is still puzzling to any reader who looks carefully, I think, because it seems to say that scientists will discover humanity's origins simply by continuing to look at "this evidence"

they already possess. What seems more likely, and what I suspect the writer means to say, is that scientists may possibly find more evidence in the future that will help them understand the past better, perhaps even unlocking the secret of humanity's origin. What kind of evidence? No doubt the kind that anthropologists uncover, since they are mentioned: ancient artifacts, human and animal remains, ancient ruins and debris.

Since the idea in the last sentence seems so directly related to the puzzle metaphor, why not continue the image all the way through? So, changing the "past in the future" phrase, making clear that there may be more evidence uncovered, adding the puzzle metaphor, we arrive at this revised sentence:

> Whether enough pieces will be found in the future to complete the puzzle and understand humanity's origin is still to be seen.

And here is the entire passage revised under the eye of our htp reader:

> Some people, including anthropologists, archaeologists, and many other scientists, believe the ancient problem of mankind's origin, a large puzzle with many missing pieces, can be solved. Though anthropologists only have bits and pieces of the whole picture today, they already can describe rather clearly man's history and development. Whether enough pieces will be found in the future to complete the puzzle and understand humanity's origin is still to be seen.

To help you appreciate the significant difference between these two passages, compare the revision to the original:

> Ever since the beginning of modern times, people have always wondered about the origin of humankind. For some, this question of ancestry is a large puzzle with many missing

pieces. For others, the solution does not seem unreachable. In fact, many feel that it is just a matter of time before man's origins are completely revealed. Among these optimistic people are anthropologists, archaeologists, and many other scientists. Though anthropologists only have various clues and guesses to work with today, they do have enough evidence to give a rather clear picture of man's history and development. Whether this evidence leads to the discovery of man's origins in the future is still to be seen.

The rewrite is not only shorter (70 words versus 113), but also tighter and therefore easier to read.

I've gone through the revision process here in considerable detail in order to show you, as much as possible, how and why it was done. Now you may feel, as you reflect on what has happened, that a tremendous amount of time and effort was needed just to revise this one paragraph. But do keep in mind that it doesn't take nearly as long to do something as it takes to describe what you're doing. Plus, some paragraphs won't need as much work; but some will need more; and some will need to be ditched entirely. The most important thing to note here is that it does take a little patience to revise successfully. Beyond that, for the most part, you just have to become a hard-to-please reader, use your common sense, and try various ways of saying something or saying something else.

Actually, you really need only to be willing to ask some basic, commonsense questions as you write and rewrite and write and rewrite and write some more:

- Is it clear? (Should it be?) Can it be clearer? (Should it be?)
- Is it concise? (Should it be?) Can it be more concise? (Should it be?)
- Is it engaging? (Should it be?) Can it be more engaging? (Should it be?)

In talking about revising, I've pretty much been pretending it is a separate step that occurs after you have a draft. And I think such an illusion is helpful, because it helps keep you from tinkering too much with what you're writing as you're first trying to get it down. But, in reality, revising occurs all along, not just as an ending activity. Writing and rewriting are pretty much indistinguishable in practice, as a writer works, even though they are usefully distinguished in theory. Revising, I would like to emphasize, is also not simply a sentence-level activity. It may involve moving whole sections around, adding or deleting support, refining or even radically altering the main point. Writing and rewriting alike involve generating possibilities and making choices; you'll make the most effective choices if you keep your options open. The bottom line, then, is that effective revision depends on a willingness to experiment, to change just about anything to see if it can't be made better. Unless you're writing in stone, it isn't written in stone—until the due date arrives.

Editing

An editor helps a writer recognize which aspects of a text are finished and which aspects need more work. Sometimes editors make suggestions and corrections themselves, but their job mainly is to bring virtues and flaws to the writer's attention.

Although most writers aren't lucky enough to have professional editors, it is nonetheless useful in some ways to think of editing and revising as separate jobs. An editor doesn't have to worry about how to fix the problems he or she finds (that's the writer's problem), and so editors may be more likely to decide this or that *is* a problem. Also, although there are always exceptions, in my experience good editors are not all that worried about the writer's ego or feelings. Their concern is with the finished product.

It doesn't really matter how long the writer worked on a piece; if it stinks, it stinks; and the writer can deal with it.

When you have a draft in pretty good shape, it's time to employ (or become) an editor. If you can get someone else to read your work, and such assistance is okay with your teacher, what should your editor look for? Anything and everything, but very simple questions—What do you like most? What do you like least? What needs more work?—can produce very useful feedback. But aside from such general concerns, there are specific stylistic flaws that good editors regularly look for.

But before we look at such flaws, a word of caution: General advice regarding style is risky, simply because an effective style is so sensitive to the particular context—the purpose, the audience, the image the writer wants to project. Good writers sometimes violate rules and principles, but they at least know they're violating them, and why.

Tightening

On a stylistic level, the editor's Prime Directive might be this: *Cut the Fat.* Editors just assume that your prose can be tighter, leaner. They try to eliminate any sentences, phrases, words, even syllables that you don't need. They want every word to earn its keep, and if a simpler word or phrase will do the same job, they want you to choose the shorter, simpler wording—unless you have a reason to do otherwise. The best writing teacher I ever had, John Trimble of the University of Texas, author of the classic *Writing with Style*, is a superb editor. John likes to count the words in the original and the revision. He likes to point out, rightly enough, that if you can tighten a 20-word sentence to 15 words, then you can cut a 200 page text to 150 pages. We'd save a lot of trees if everyone edited so astutely.

How do you find the flab to cut? Here are some tips to help you.

• *Look at the subjects of your sentences.* Is every one *really* the proper subject? That is, does the subject of each sentence accurately reflect its focus? Are you saying "The kind of situation involved here is one of miscommunication between the engineer and the architect"? Or, are you putting the real actor and action in the subject and verb positions, as in "The architect misled the engineer"? Richard Lanham's *Revising Prose* (or *Revising Business Prose,* if you prefer marketplace examples) can provide extensively detailed help on getting the parts of your sentences organized. A few examples, however, can illustrate much of Lanham's method, I think.

The following sentences are adapted from an essay discussing waste disposal problems (by Elizabeth Royte, in *Harper's,* June 1992). Consider this one:

> The situation is one in which still more landfills will be forced to close, following the EPA requirements introduced last September.

Although it is possible that the "situation" is where the writer actually wants the focus, it seems unlikely. The real subject of the sentence, I would suggest, is either "more landfills" or "EPA requirements." To decide which one to use, you'd need to look at the context in which the sentence occurs. Notice how changing the subject changes the sentence in each case:

> More landfills will be forced to close, following the EPA requirements introduced last September.

> EPA requirements introduced last September will force still more landfills to close. (Royte's actual version)

Notice that the first version has 22 words; the second has 14; and the third has 11, which is cutting the original in half. Imagine if everything you read were half as long as it is, if your physics text were 125 pages instead of 250, if your IRS instructions were 8 pages instead of 16!

Some sentences begin not with the wrong subject, but without one—or with a subject that is essentially empty:

There are scarred hillsides of this valley that provide a good vantage point from which to view the nation's garbage wars.

The first word here, "There," is just a pointing word, linked by "are" to the rest of the sentence. Sometimes you do want simply to point out a situation or a fact, and beginning with "There are" or "It is" is a good idea. But oftentimes the sentence will seem more effective, not to mention more direct, when the subject position is occupied by a real subject:

Scarred hillsides of this valley provide a good vantage point from which to view the nation's garbage.

• *Look for phrases that can be replaced by a word or at least a shorter phrase.* Consider, for example, this sentence: "The shift in voter loyalty is due to the fact that the economy grew even worse." Is there a familiar phrase in this sentence? Yes, of course, it's "due to the fact that." What happens if you try to replace that phrase?

The shift in voter loyalty occurred because the economy grew even worse.

Or, changing the subject of the sentence, we have this leaner and more direct version:

Voter loyalty shifted because the economy grew even worse.

• *Look for prepositional phrases that can be collapsed or eliminated*, especially where you have a string of prepositional phrases. For instance: "The imbalance of chemicals in the liver of the patient caused problems for the intern of the evening watch." If we try to remove some of the prepositional phrases, what happens?

The chemical imbalance in the patient's liver caused problems for the evening-watch intern.

We've gone here from 19 words to 14, making the sentence a little tighter. (You may want to consult the section on hyphens, especially if you don't fully understand why "evening-watch" is hyphenated here.)

• ***Watch out for large words and stilted phrasings.*** One clue to wordiness may be the flowering of words ending in *-ion*. For instance: "The institution told those directly involved in the educational profession that consultation would be forthcoming." I think this sentence means simply:

> "The administrators told the teachers they would be consulted."

That's 15 words converted to 9—saving over a third. Plus, the revision just sounds friendlier, more like a person talking. If you cannot imagine yourself saying what you've written, then ask yourself how you would say it. Then write that down and revise it rather than the original written version.

Here are some other examples and revisions (see if you can explain the principles behind the revisions):

Original #1

It is largely because of the fact that Grant caused such widespread destruction that many Southerners dislike the North even to the present time.

Revision #1

Grant caused such widespread destruction that many Southerners dislike the North even today.

Or,

Many Southerners dislike the North even today because Grant caused such widespread destruction.

Original #2

In the event that a hurricane hits Charleston again, the new construction regulations will have been applied for the purpose of making buildings stronger.

Revision #2

If a hurricane hits Charleston again, the new building codes to make buildings stronger will have been applied.

Original #3

If economists take into consideration only the purchasing capability of Argentinians of the upper class, the recent period of inflation in the double digits will seem rather mild.

Revision #3

If economists consider only the buying power of upper-class Argentinians, the recent period of double-digit inflation will seem rather mild.

Enlivening

Editors also look for opportunities to make writing style livelier, more vigorous, more appealing. What makes prose more engaging? Try some of the following (but not all at once in every sentence!):

• *Include comparisons.* Ask yourself, "What is this like?" When the U.S. Army was debating whether to hire Indian warriors to track and catch Apache warriors like Geronimo, one officer said, "Using standard methods is like trying to hunt down a deer with a marching band." The comparison made the case powerfully, and the Indian scouts were hired. (Too bad an equally eloqent spokesman wasn't around to speak for the Apaches.) In his "Travels in Georgia," John McPhee talks about a turtle that was "run over like a manhole cover, probably with much the same sound." When a sheriff puts the turtle out of its misery, McPhee says "the gun made an absurdly light sound, like a screen door shutting." A friend of McPhee's carries the dead turtle down to the pond "like a heavy suitcase with a broken strap." These comparisons bring the idea to life, making us see one thing in terms of another, enriching our grasp. "Oh, so *that's* what it sounded like," we say. (As you may know, when you use "like" or "as," the comparison is called a "simile." If you don't use "like" or "as," it is known as a "metaphor.")

• **Replace weak verbs** with more active, more vivid, more precise verbs. Instead of saying "he walked slowly along," you might want to say "he *meandered* along." Instead of "the new recipe is better than the old one," you might want to say, "the new recipe grabs your taste buds, while the old one just teased them." Most teachers and style guides will tell you to watch out for "to be" or linking verbs: "is," "are," "am," "was." These verbs certainly are useful, and oftentimes they are fine to use. But when most of your sentences simply say that "X is Y," then it is likely that your prose is not very vivid or active. So, as you're revising, see if some of your linking verbs should be converted.

• **Add details.** Perhaps "She went to work" should be changed to "Mary Catherine crawled out of bed and stumbled over to her computer, determined to write up the annual report despite her mind-boggling hangover." One of the most common student shortcomings in writing classes is saying too little, taking for granted that the reader can see or understand whatever is clear to the writer.

One effective way to add details is to use appositives. An "appositive" adds information by renaming a noun: Instead of "Samuel Johnson said many witty things," you write "Samuel Johnson, the eighteenth-century author, said many witty things." Or, going further, you might say "Samuel Johnson, the eighteenth-century author, the subject of Boswell's great biography, said many witty things."

• ***Be specific.*** Instead of "After a boring day, he went home," you might want to say this: "After a lengthy and lumbering discussion of the toilet paper allotment, an unnecessary and uneventful meeting with his assistant, and four hours of staring out his window at the building next door, he went home."

• ***Use a few startlingly short sentences,*** even one- or two-word sentences. Absolutely. (Just like that; and also try some parenthetical comments on what you've just said.) Also try some dashes, semicolons, and colons. Bullet dots are also effective when you want to list items. These are the sorts of things magazine writers do to liven up the page. Look closely at writing that aspires to be popular and try to do what you see those writers doing, even at the level of punctuation.

Connecting

Good writing flows. Readers like to find themselves moving smoothly along, as each sentence seems to be connected to the preceding sentences. This connectedness is often referred to as "coherence," the property of bonding together. Good editors are on the lookout for gaps in coherence. A number of strategies contribute to this quality, which some readers refer to as "flowing"; mainly you want to link every sentence in some way to what has gone before and what is coming next. To see how a passage holds together, let's look at an example, by Francis Davis:

> What used to appeal to listeners, both black and white, about black performers like James Brown, Ray Charles, Aretha Franklin, and even such Motown smoothies as Marvin Gaye and Smokey Robinson, was their "authenticity," the indisputable realness of their music and the cultural values it embodied. By comparison, recent black performers, including the comic-strip militants Public Enemy, have transformed themselves into self-caricatures as insubstantial as the "Toons" in the 1988 movie *Who Framed Roger*

Rabbit?, who were understood to be standing in for racial minorities. A glance at any Guns N' Roses video should be enough to persuade us that black performers aren't contemporary pop's only Toons. But because pop music plays such a large part in shaping both black self-image and white perceptions of black culture, more is at stake in the persona of a performer who is black.

—Francis Davis, "Toons," in *The Atlantic,* April 1992

What features of coherent writing can we notice here?

First, coherent writing often involves repeating words and phrases, or using synonyms, antonyms, or other variations of words. Such repetition keeps the reader's attention focused on the subject. In Davis's passage, notice how the repetition of the word "black" in every sentence helps to link the sentences together: the paragraph focuses on what "black" means. Also, notice how "realness" is contrasted to "Toons" (a cartoon being of course the opposite of real). This opposition also helps knit the passage together.

Second, coherent writing often involves using pronouns and pointing adjectives. In the example above, notice how "their" and "themselves" help to create coherence. Third, coherent writing often involves repeating a construction or phrase. The phrase "black performers," for instance, reappears in the passage above. Fourth, coherent writing often involves explicit transitions. In Davis's example, "By comparison" and "But" point out relationships.

Of course, using any sort of technique to improve your coherence will be ineffective if your thinking is not coherent. As you're drafting, it is inevitable that ideas will interrupt the progression of your thought, taking you down tangential lines of development, leading you to associate the current topic with some other. In editing, you'll want to look for these distracting or interrupting ideas and to revise them by grouping related ideas together. Coherent writing (usually) doesn't require the reader to make leaps of logic or to fill in narrative omissions. The writing goes step by step, as sentences are linked and related.

Once you're satisfied the ideas really do fit together and are in the proper order, then you want to make sure the reader is able to see the progression. Here is a brief guide to some explicit connecting devices:

✦ *Tips for Coherent Writing*

- Similar ideas can be explicitly connected by "likewise," "similarly," "by the same token," "in the same way," and "also."

- Contrasting ideas can be explicitly connected by "but," "yet," "however," "still," "even so," "on the other hand," and several other connectors.

- Items in sequence can be explicitly connected by numerical ordering: "first," "second," "third," and so on.

- An idea can be connected to preceding material by being simply added to it, using "and," "in addition," "furthermore," "also," "besides," and other linking words.

- An idea that acknowledges what your reader already knows, or that there are other points of view, can be explicitly connected by "of course," "granted," "to be sure," "even though," and other words.

- Illustrations can be explicitly connected by "for example," "for instance," and "in particular."

- Conclusions can be explicitly linked by "therefore," "thus," "hence," "consequently," and other words.

Notice how many of the features just mentioned contribute to the coherence of the following paragraph, from "The Next New Deal" by Neil Howe and Phillip Longman:

> Finally, there was the program originally designed to offer all Americans what President Franklin Roosevelt's brain trusters called "a floor of protection" against destitution in old age. But over the course of more than half a century Social Security had evolved into something radically different. By 1991 the system was distributing more than $55 billion a year, or more than a fifth of its benefits, to househoolds with incomes above $50,000. For that much money the government could have provided every American with cradle-to-grave insurance against poverty— including the one American child in twenty who lived in a household reporting a cash income during 1991 of less than $5,000.
>
> —*The Atlantic,* April 1992

Proofing

You've written and rewritten and edited and rewritten and written some more, and now your text is finished. Yet, there is one more thing you need to do—and then you might need to do some more. You need to proofread your text, catching errors and infelicities, large and small, before they slip into print.

One of the difficulties in proofreading, however, once you've decided to do it, is that the paper is so familiar to you that you see what you think it says, not what is really on the page. A cure for this problem is to read the paper backwards, proofreading the last sentence first, then the next-to-last sentence, and so forth. That way, it's harder for you think about what the text is saying, and you're more likely to look at its mechanics—the spelling, the grammar, the complete thoughts, and such. You can also tell a good bit by reading your paper aloud. This strategy isn't as helpful for finding typing or spelling errors, but it helps you determine if sentences make sense and sound okay.

It's much better to make marks on your final copy, correcting errors or clearing up obscurities, than to turn in a beautiful paper with errors and obscurities remaining. It would be nice if you could catch those problems before you print out or type up the final version, but most people do not mind edited copy—as long as the changes aren't too numerous or too messy. Very few manuscripts sent to publishers are typed perfectly; and if they are, the publishers' editors will very quickly make a mess of them anyway, adding questions, marking the copy for the printer, making suggestions and corrections.

Plus, your reader or teacher is almost certainly going to write on your paper, perhaps making some of the same corrections you might make. So, save your reader this trouble and aggravation: proofread and edit your final copy, and don't hesitate to make marks on it. You're not in a typing course. (Unless, of course, you are, or your teacher tells you otherwise.)

For proofreading texts, writers and editors have evolved over the years certain symbols. The marks shown in Figure 4.1 are taken from *Webster's Ninth Collegiate Dictionary*, but these are standard: editors around the world recognize these symbols. The most useful ones are those for deleting, adding, and letting something stand in the original version after it has been changed. You should memorize these symbols and practice using them.

Format and Appearance

Common sense will help you here. You want the paper to make a good impression, so what will accomplish that? It should be easy to read, and what you're saying should be the focus. Make sure you use a sharp ribbon. If you're using a dot-matrix printer, be sure to use the letter-quality setting, or at least double-strike or bold. Don't make your reader strain to see what you're saying (after dozens of

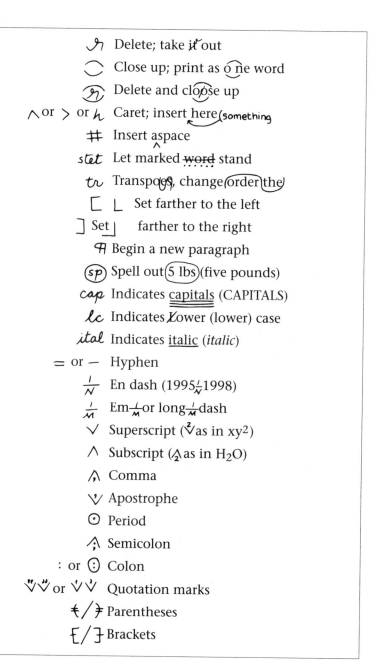

◆ **Figure 4.1** Proofreaders' Marks

papers, small difficulties start to seem larger). Make all corrections clearly, with black or blue-black ink. If you're writing by hand, use your best handwriting, and skip lines.

About the paper: don't use onion-skin paper. It tends to float off the table with the least little breeze. Also, don't use a colored paper. Just plain white is strongly preferred. Follow whatever directions your teacher or supervisor or project leader has given you about the format, but be sure to put your name and the page number on every page. Also, a date on the first page is nice (that way, your grandchildren will know when you wrote your masterpiece). It's also helpful to include information about the course, just in case the paper gets separated from you or your teacher. (See the sample first page below.)

Jacob Schimpf
Professor Lindstedt
Paper #1
September 25, 1996

You should also make sure you have an effective title. All too often, students omit titles for their essays, or call them "Paper #2" or something equally unrevealing and unappealing. A title like "Melville's *Moby Dick*" or "Pope's *Dunciad*," for instance, tells the reader very little. Is the novel itself going to follow? Will the essay cover every possible aspect of the novel? Also, notice that the actual title is not enclosed in quotation marks unless it is a quotation; when you refer to a title, of course, you do use quotation marks in order to tell the reader, "This is the actual title, so I'm using the author's words, so it's in quotation marks." Most teachers do not want a cover sheet with only the title and your name. So the first page of a paper, usually, will look something like this:

Jacob Schimpf
Professor Lindstedt
Paper #1
September 25, 1996

Blowing Smoke:
Cigarette Advertising and Health Issues

Tesifying recently before the U.S. Occupational
Safety and Health Administration (OSHA), an environmental health expert noted that a non-smoker who
works for one month near one smoker takes in as much
NDMA, which is a particularly potent cancer-causing
compound, as someone who has smoked 75 cigarettes.[1]
But the R. J. Reynolds Company's recent advertising

And here's how the second page might look:

Schimpf 2

while "sidestream" smoke, the technical term for the
smoke that curls off the end of a burning cigarette, con-
tains higher levels of carcinogens than the "main-
stream" smoke that is exhaled by the smoker.

I'd like to emphasize here the importance of having a meaningful title. It's not just a formality; titles are very powerful. As your
own experience as a reader will no doubt indicate, the title of a
piece often determines whether you will read it. Perhaps students
often ignore titles because they know that in a school setting the

reader usually feels compelled to read what they have written no matter what. But it is certainly to your benefit even in such compulsory situations if the reader *wants* to read what you've written.

The title not only can draw readers in, but it also can prepare them for what is to follow. In some recent issues of *Esquire*, a magazine consistently noted for excellent writing, the following titles appear: "A Nation of Crybabies: What Japan Thinks of Us"; "Rocket Launches, Lust, Croquet, and the Fall of the West"; and "Inhuman Architecture, Bad Food, Boredom, and Death by Fun and Games." These titles range from being fairly descriptive ("What Japan Thinks of Us") to intriguingly strange (what do rocket launches, lust, and croquet have to do with the fall of the West?). They are designed to grab a reader's attention with odd juxtapositions and striking assertions.

In some contexts, however, your title should be entirely informational. The third quarter report for your company shouldn't be called "Trouble in Paradise" or "We're in the Money." Instead, "Reorganization Planned" or "Dramatic Increases in Earnings" would be more appropriate.

In your English classes, especially when you are writing argumentative essays (about literature or any other topic), your title should probably be informative and engaging but not cute. For instance, an article by Marshall Brown in *PMLA*, by some accounts the leading journal of literary scholarship, is called "Unheard Melodies: The Force of Form." The first part of the title is an allusion (an implied reference, specifically to these lines in Keats's *Ode on a Grecian Urn*: "Heard melodies are sweet, but those unheard/ Are sweeter"). Brown's use of this line is interesting because "form" is a part of a work that is not "heard." It is the arrangement of the parts, not their expression; form is an abstraction. Brown's title is then descriptive and interesting. This kind of two-part title that Brown uses appears fairly often, especially in academic discourse: one part (usually the first) provides an engaging and suggestive hook; the other part, usually following a colon, provides more information.

How can you find a good title? Your first resource is the paper itself. Is there perhaps a quotation that has a phrase you can use in your title? Is there a sentence of your own that can be converted into the title? Titles are often in one way or another responses to other works and their titles, so the more widely you read, the more materials you can draw on for your title.

For your convenience, here's a countdown checklist before your paper leaves the launchpad.

✦ *Paper Blast-Off Checklist*

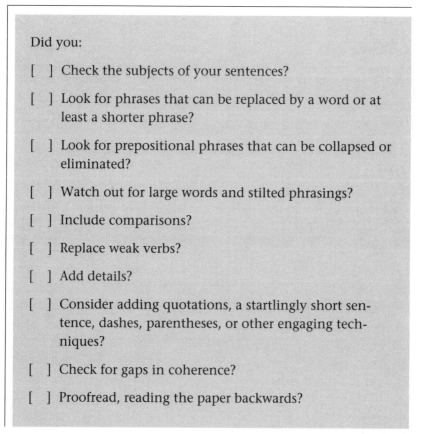

Did you:

[ ] Check the subjects of your sentences?

[ ] Look for phrases that can be replaced by a word or at least a shorter phrase?

[ ] Look for prepositional phrases that can be collapsed or eliminated?

[ ] Watch out for large words and stilted phrasings?

[ ] Include comparisons?

[ ] Replace weak verbs?

[ ] Add details?

[ ] Consider adding quotations, a startlingly short sentence, dashes, parentheses, or other engaging techniques?

[ ] Check for gaps in coherence?

[ ] Proofread, reading the paper backwards?

(continued)

[   ] Use proofreader's marks?

[   ] Make sure the paper is easy to read (lines are skipped, plain white paper is used)?

[   ] Follow the assigned or appropriate format?

[   ] Use an effective title?

[   ] Have a chocolate-chip cookie (or other suitable indulgence) to celebrate?

5

Usage and Abusage

"Whom are you," he said, for he had been to night school.

—George Ade

♦ ♦ ♦

A User-Friendly Grammar

In many English classes students are required to purchase a grammar handbook. The size of these books testifies to the difficulties of mastering something as complex and strange as a language—especially one as diverse and rich as English. Even if a handbook is not required, you will find one helpful as a resource. This chapter will offer a condensed version of a grammar handbook, allowing you to review quickly the basics and to assess for yourself what you need to work on, using a handbook and other resources discussed next. In a sense, what follows is then both an abbreviated handbook and a guide to handbooks.

The Sentence

A sentence, the conventional definition tells us, is "a group of words expressing a complete thought." For a thought to be complete, it must have a subject and a verb. One of these can be understood, and so a sentence can be one word: "Come." "Me." In the first, perhaps "you" is understood: "You come." And in the second perhaps "She should give it to" is understood: "She should give it to me." So, whenever a sentence is incomplete, it must exist in a context that implies the missing element, whether subject or verb.

Taken together, a subject and verb constitute a clause. A sentence thus must have at least one clause, but it can have more than one. Clauses that can stand alone as sentences are called "main clauses." Clauses that cannot stand alone, that seem incomplete by themselves, are called "dependent clauses" because they are *dependent* on something else to make complete sense.

Here's an independent clause:

Governor Filbert offered the bill.

This makes sense by itself. "Governor Filbert" is the subject; "offered" is the verb.

Here's a dependent clause:

Although Governor Filbert offered the bill.

This doesn't make sense by itself. It isn't a sentence.

In both of these clauses, "the bill" is what is called a "direct object," the recipient of the verb's action.

It is possible to have an "indirect object" if the verb describes some kind of "giving" action.

Governor Filbert offered local officials the bill.
      Subject   *Verb*   *Indirect Object*   *Direct Object*

In simple sentences, the subject comes first. But the subject can appear in various positions, of course, and any number of independent and dependent clauses can appear.

Although no one appreciated the gesture, Governor Filbert offered the bill.

Governor Filbert, even though no one appreciated the gesture, offered the bill, and then he quickly flew to Washington.

No one appreciated the gesture, but Governor Filbert offered the bill anyway, and then he quickly flew to Washington.

Ordinarily, writers put the most important information in the main clauses, and supporting material in the dependent clauses. This convention can be violated with comic effect:

Although she is a thief, a traitor, and a child abuser, she is an excellent typist.

Parts of Speech

• *Noun.* A noun names something—a person, a place, an object, an idea, anything. A proper noun names a specific thing and is capitalized—Shakespeare; Greer, S.C.; the Atlanta Braves.

• *Verb.* Verbs are the engines of sentences. They convey the action. In some cases that action is a state of being, indicated by "to be" or linking verbs ("is," "was," "are," "were," "became," "remains," and others).

• *Pronoun.* A pronoun stands for a noun. In "The children went out to play, but they will be back soon," the word "children" is the noun, and "they" is the pronoun, substituting for the noun.

• *Adjective.* An adjective adds information to a noun, "modifying" it, as we usually say. Adding an adjective to "the outfielder," we get "the agile outfielder."

• *Adverb.* An adverb modifies a verb, or another adverb, or an adjective.

The cake rose *beautifully*.   [modifying the verb]

The cake rose *very* beautifully.   [modifying the other adverb]

The *beautifully* rising cake was chocolate.   [modifying an adjective]

• *Preposition.* A preposition links a noun or pronoun to a sentence, showing relationship, placing the noun or pronoun in time and space. Words like "of," "around," "to," and "on" are prepositions.

• *Conjunction.* A conjunction joins sentences, clauses, phrases, or even words. "And," "but," "because," and "unless" are all conjunctions. One kind of conjunction that appears in a pair is called a coordinating conjunction (for instance, "both/and" or "either/or").

Pronouns

Let's talk about some common problems with pronouns.

Subjective, Objective, Possessive

Pronouns come in three "cases": subjective, objective, and possessive. For the first-person pronoun, these three cases are "I," "me," and "my" or "mine."

Subjective: *I* played the Mozart piece last night.

Objective: The Mozart piece was played last night by *me*.

Possessive: *My* version of the Mozart piece was played last night.

These cases usually don't cause problems except in the following circumstances:

• *Compound Subjects.* Most people would not say "Me have a new house." But a surprising number of people would say "Jane and me have a new house." Whether a sentence has a single subject or a compound subject, the pronoun should be in the subjective case: I, you, he, she, it, we, they, who, whoever.

• *Compound Objects.* Likewise, to most people, "The rocks hit I" sounds wrong. But "The rocks hit Jane and I" apparently sounds fine to many people. So, whenever you have a compound object or subject including a pronoun, eliminate the other subject to see which case to use. If the pronoun is in the object position, receiving the action of the verb, or serving as the object of a preposition, then use the objective case: me, you, him, her, it, us, them, whom, whomever.

• *Predicate Nominatives.* In the following sentence "Valerie and I" is a predicate nominative:

The leaders of the group are Valerie and I.

In sentences with linking verbs, like "are," the predicate of the sentence takes the subjective case: it is being equated with the subject. Admittedly, this practice does sound a little odd to many people:

The teachers are Laura and she.

And in informal usage, most people accept the use of the objective case of the pronoun after a linking verb:

It is I.   [formally correct]

It is me.   [informally accepted]

• *Other Instances.* After "than" or "as," use the pronoun case as if the sentence were completed:

Annette is smarter than I.   [". . . smarter than I am."]

Jane cannot eat as much as he.   [". . . as much as he can eat."]

An appositive renames a noun. When a pronoun appears in an appositive, use the same case as the noun being renamed:

The full partners—Jack, Sally, and I—are going to Mexico.

"Who" and "Whom"

Many Americans never use "whom" and rely instead on "who" exclusively. Other people, aware that "who" and "whom" are troublesome words, assume that whatever sounds right to them must be wrong and therefore "correct" their speech to the wrong form. For informal usage, "who" is acceptable to most people, but in writing you want to have the correct form. And unless you perceive it will sound stuffy or stilted, you might as well have the correct form in speech. It really isn't that difficult.

Probably all you need to do is substitute another personal pronoun for "who" or "whom" (or for "whoever" or "whomever"—same rules apply). For instance:

Is it "*Who* shall I say is calling?" Or "*Whom* shall I say is calling?"

Since it's easier to deal with statements rather than questions, first turn the question into a statement: "I shall say who/whom is calling." If we substitute another personal pronoun, see which of these sounds better:

I shall say her is calling.

I shall say she is calling.

To almost every native speaker of English, "she is calling" sounds much better. "She" is, of course, the subjective form, corresponding to "who," so "Who shall I say is calling?" is right.

Here's another example:

Tom was not who/whom the new teacher asked.

In this case, you need to take the sentence apart enough to see what role "who" or "whom" plays. As it turns out, "who" or "whom" is the object of the verb "asked": "the new teacher asked who/whom." And which of these sounds better?

The new teacher asked her.

The new teacher asked she.

"Her," the objective case, sounds better; so "whom" is the right choice. Whenever "who" or "whom" appears in a dependent clause, just remove the clause from the sentence and rearrange it to see what role "who" or "whom" plays.

"We" and "Us"

Again, these two pronouns seem to give most people trouble only in certain situations. In this case, many people have trouble when "we" or "us" is used together with a noun, as in the following sentence:

We/Us English teachers have to stick together.

The trick to determining which form to use is simply to remove the noun. Decide which sounds better: "We must stick together" or "Us must stick together." Clearly, to most native speakers, the first sounds better because it is the correct form for a subject.

How about this sentence?

Clinton really laid it on we/us Republicans.

Again, do you prefer "on us" or "on we"? "On us" sounds much better to most native speakers. Hence, it's correct.

"He" (Avoiding Sexist Speech)

Some writers believe it is defensible to use "he" as an inclusive pronoun, to use "mankind" as a term that includes both men and women, and to begin a letter with "Dear Sir" even though the sex of the person who will receive it is unknown, and many other related usages. It is true that for decades, even centuries, these have been conventional in our language. Only in the past few decades has their unfairness and narrowmindedness become increasingly evident. If one were to suggest that "she" includes both men and women, the idea would immediately seem absurd. Why should "he" be different? The Dean of the Medical School who wants to thank at graduation "all the supportive wives of our new doctors" is obviously out of touch since over a third of today's medical students are women. Likewise, referring generically to a nurse as "she" makes no sense: nurses come in both sexes today.

We all need to become sensitive to the way we use language because words do convey power. They reinforce prejudices—sometimes in subtle ways, sometimes blatantly. Here are some tips on avoiding sexist language.

✦ *Tips on Avoiding Sexist Language*

- Use plural forms.

  Instead of:

  > An engineer must pass his certification exam.

  Use:

  > Engineers must pass their certification exams.

- Eliminate the pronoun.

  > An engineer must pass a certification exam.

- Use "he or she," or "him or her."

  > An engineer must pass his or her certification exam.

- Use another word that is not gendered.

  Instead of "fireman," for instance, use "firefighter." Instead of "chairman," use "chair." Instead of "mailman," use "mail carrier." Instead of "mankind," use "humanity."

Adjectives and Adverbs

Adjectives and adverbs expand our experience of words, adding to nouns and verbs, refining and sharpening what a writer says. In this passage from Edgar Allan Poe's classic story, "The Tell-Tale Heart," notice the important role of the adjectives (which modify nouns and pronouns) and the adverbs (which modify verbs, adjectives, and other adverbs):

> Presently I heard a slight groan, and I knew it was the groan of mortal terror. It was not a groan of pain or of grief—oh, no!—it was the low stifled sound that arises from the bottom of the soul when overcharged with awe. I knew the sound very well. Many a night, just at midnight, when all the world slept, it has welled up from my own bosom, with its dreadful echo, the terrors that distracted me.

Poe does not overburden this passage with modification, but the adjectives and adverbs he does use make a difference—the difference between a groan and a slight groan, between knowing a sound and knowing it very well.

In addition to encouraging you to use adjectives and adverbs, this section covers the most common problems students have with them. If you can distinguish between adjectives and adverbs, you can solve just about any usage problem involving adverbs and adjectives. Remember that adjectives modify nouns and pronouns, and adverbs modify verbs, adjectives, and other adverbs. Adjectives answer the following questions: Which? How many? What kind? Adverbs answer these questions: How? When? Where? To what extent?

Now, look at these two sentences. Which is right?

I feel bad.
I feel badly.

How can you tell? Does "badly," the adverb, belong to the verb, modifying the action of feeling? Or does "bad," the adjective, belong to the subject? Many people say "I feel badly," but that sentence actually means that their ability to sense things physically, to feel, is poor. "I feel bad" is probably what the speaker means to say. The verb "feel" links the subject to the modifier. "Bad" refers to the speaker's condition—what kind of condition he or she is in.

To understand this distinction better, consider the difference in these two sentences:

The quarterback looked cautious.

The quarterback looked cautiously at the linebackers.

In the first version, "looked" functions as a linking verb, calling for the adjective "cautious." In the second version, "looked" is an action verb, calling for the adverb form.

Another example:

He always dresses formal.

He always dresses formally.

In this case, "formally" modifies "dresses," so the adverb form, "formally," is correct.

One more:

The pizza tasted bad.

The pizza tasted badly.

"Tasted" here must be a linking verb. If it is an action verb, then pizza must have the capability to taste, and as an inanimate object, pizza can't taste. "Bad," the adjective form, is correct.

A final word about adjectives and adverbs: In conversation, "real" is often used for "really." Be careful in writing, however, to distinguish between the two. It's incorrect to say "We were real happy with our room." Instead, "we were really happy with our room" is correct.

Verbs

Kinds of Verbs

In this section, I will not try to cover every distinction that can be made about verbs. Instead, I will focus on those kinds that you need to understand in order to make the most of some important advice.

Action versus State-of-Being Verbs. Verbs are divided into *action verbs* and *state-of-being verbs*. State-of-being verbs, like "is," "was," "are," "were," are sometimes overused by writers. *Try to use your verbs to show the reader some action, which is usually more engaging and revealing than simply linking subject and predicate.*
Compare:

Willie Mays was a good hitter of high fastballs.

Willie Mays slugged high fastballs.

There are, of course, times when "to be" verbs are exactly what you need. The best advice is simply to notice when you use a state-of-being verb and consider if an action verb would be better.

Transitive versus Intransitive Verbs. Action verbs are divided into transitive (those that take objects) and intransitive (those that don't have objects).
Example:

President Kennedy believed the story of his assistant.
[transitive]

Although many doubted, President Kennedy believed.
[intransitive]

If the subject of a transitive verb is *not* the agent but rather the recipient of the verb's action, then the verb is said to be "passive," or in the passive voice. If the subject does perform the action, then the verb is "active."

> Kennedy believed the assistant.　[active, transitive]
>
> The assistant was believed by Kennedy.　[passive, transitive]

Although some students are occasionally told "avoid passive voice," such advice is too simple. You should, to be sure, *try to make most of your verbs active, using passive verbs only when you have a reason to use them.* Passive verbs are fine—indeed, they're very effective—when you want to emphasize the passivity of the subject. "I was hit by a train" focuses the attention on me as the recipient of the train's action. "A train hit me" shifts the emphasis to the train and offers a different meaning. Passive verbs are also fine when the agent is unknown or unimportant. In much scientific writing, such use of the passive voice is common. It doesn't matter who held the test tube; it only matters that the chlorine is poured into it. The statement "The test tube was filled with chlorine" focuses our attention differently from "Sam filled the test tube with chlorine."

Verb Tenses.　English has three major tenses: present, past, and future. You want to understand these tenses because you want to keep the reader oriented in time, and verb tense is crucial to that orientation. More on this in a moment.

Present tense describes conditions now, which can include timeless events:

> My aunt is happy to come.
>
> The newscaster takes the microphone.
>
> A virus mutates under stress.

Events that occur in literary works are usually described in present tense:

Flem Snopes auctions off a diseased horse in the opening scene.

Past tense conveys events that have occurred or conditions that did exist:

My aunt was happy to come.

The virus mutated under stress.

Future tense tells about events or conditions to come:

My aunt will be happy to come.

The virus will mutate under stress.

Each of the major tenses has a "perfect" form. Present perfect tense conveys that the events or conditions began in the past and may still continue to the present:

My aunt has been happy to come.

The virus has mutated under stress.

Past perfect tense tells us about an event or condition that occurred in the past and does not extend into the present:

My aunt had been happy to come.

The virus had mutated under stress.

Future perfect tense depicts an event or condition that will occur in the future and then end:

My aunt will have been happy to come.

The virus will have mutated under stress.

Keeping your reader oriented in time does not mean that every verb is in the same tense. It means that your position in time remains stable. Consider how this paragraph shifts about in its orientation:

> At the news conference, the chief researcher says his resignation was ready. He said the problem is not his fault, however. He thinks the media has been unfair. He wanted everyone to continue to support the center.

It's difficult to tell if the reader is supposed to be situated in the present, looking back at a news conference in the past, or if the reader is supposed to be experiencing the news conference in the present tense.

Subjunctive versus Indicative Verbs. If the verb describes a condition that is not true, that is contrary to the facts, then the mood of the verb is said to be "subjunctive," which is distinguished from the ordinary mood of verbs, indicative. For instance, if I say "If I were king," I am stating a condition that is not (alas) true. In the indicative mood, I would say "I was king"—which is entirely different. Of course, the second is also untrue, but my statement doesn't indicate this condition. You may need to study how the "to be" verbs change from indicative to subjunctive.

Indicative		Subjunctive	
Present			
I am	we are	(if) I be	(if) we be
you are	you are	(if) you be	(if) you be
he/she/it is	they are	(if) he/she/it be	(if) they be
Past			
I was	we were	(if) I were	(if) we were
you were	you were	(if) you were	(if) you were
he/she/it was	they were	(if) he/she/it were	(if) they were

Troublesome Verbs

Some verbs just hang around seedy pool halls, flashing their tatoos, fingering their sharp knives, picking their decaying teeth. They're trouble. But the most troublesome are probably "lie" and "lay," or "sit" and "set." If no one knew which one of these pairs to use, things would be okay; but there are people who know, and many of them are irritated or shocked by those who don't. So you might as well learn which verb to use, and be one of those people in the know. It's really not that confusing, and there's a certain satisfaction in knowing you're using the right word.

Lie or Lay.   Focus on these two sentences:

I'm going to lie down.

I'm going to lay the book down.

"Lie" means to recline—to lie down. "Lay" means to place—to lay something down. So "lie" is intransitive, not taking an object. "Lay" is transitive, taking an object.

This distinction is, I think, easy enough to keep straight. The difficulty lies in the various tenses. Study how the tenses change the verbs. You'll just have to memorize these changes:

I'm going to lie down.

I lay down yesterday.

I have lain down everyday.

I have been lying down everyday.

I'm going to lay the book down.

I laid the book down yesterday.

I have laid the book down everyday.

I have been laying the book down everyday.

Sit or Set. "Set" means "to place." "Sit" means "to be seated." Here's how these two verbs change:

I'm going to sit here.

I sat here yesterday.

I have sat here everyday.

I have been sitting here everyday.

I'm going to set the book here.

I set the book here yesterday.

I have set the book here everyday.

I have been setting the book here everyday.

Agreement

Probably the most troublesome agreement problem for most students stems from the way the verb *to be* changes. If the following constructions don't sound natural to you, study them, use them in sentences, and recite them until they do:

Present Tense

Singular	*Plural*
I am	we are
you are	you are
he/she/it is	they are

Past Tense

Singular	*Plural*
I was	we were
you were	you were
he/she/it was	they were

Other agreement problems may arise when writers neglect to add -s or -es to the verb ending when there's a third-person singular:

I smell good.

You smell good.

He *smells* good.

I hit the ball.

You hit the ball.

She *hits* the ball.

Also, if the subject is compound and joined by "or" or "nor," then make the verb agree with the subject closer to it:

Paul or the other Beatles have performed there, but not both.

Neither the brothers nor the father was there.

Finally, watch out for phrases that come between the subject and verb; it's easy to forget what the subject really is, and make the verb mistakenly agree with a noun near it.

The girls, together with their horse, are going to be in town.

Punctuation

The Comma

More men came behind them, dressed in work clothes, carrying folding chairs, black trunklike boxes with silver hinges, microphones, a wooden lectern, and an armload of bunting.

—Anne Tyler

If you think there are firm rules that cover every punctuating situation, that for any particular thing you want to say there's only one way to punctuate it, then you are in for a world of frustration and anxiety. We really don't have zillions of punctuation rules governing every contingency. Instead, we have some general guidelines that writers apply as they see fit. The essential thing to understand is what a comma does: It signals a pause. It doesn't separate things firmly saying "this is different"; instead, the comma says "what's coming next is related to what you've just read—it's just a different part." In Tyler's sentence, the comma organizes the details—here one detail ends, the next begins—but it doesn't isolate them. Each detail is part of the whole picture of the sentence.

You probably need a comma anywhere you would pause as you read your writing aloud. If you need to indicate a stop, to signal the end of one thought and the beginning of another, you need something stronger than a comma: a connecting word like "and" or "but" added to the comma; or a semicolon; or a colon; or a dash; or a period.

There are, to be sure, a few major conventions that you violate at your peril. Otherwise, there's considerable leeway for your judgment.

Here are the most important things to watch out for with a comma.

• Don't use only a comma to separate two independent clauses. This error, often called a comma splice, is considered major by virtually every writing teacher. Why? What's the big deal? First, let's look at an example of the error:

> I have been to see the new dealership, with money in my pocket I felt like a deer on the first day of hunting season.

As experienced readers move through this sentence, they are likely to believe they are reading this sentence:

> I have been to see the new dealership, with money in my pocket. . . .

The problem is that the sentence goes on past "pocket" until it is obvious that another sentence is coming up with "I felt." At this point, the reader has to drop whatever assumptions have been made and rethink the structure of the sentence. So, the reason a comma splice is such a major error is that it often sends misleading signals to readers, confusing them and requiring them to go back and correct their understanding.

Avoiding comma splices is easy enough:

1. Add a connecting word: "I have been to see the new dealership, but with money in my pocket I felt like a deer on the first day of hunting season."

2. Or, use another mark of punctuation to separate the two sentences: "I have been to see the new dealership; with money in my pocket I felt like a deer on the first day of hunting season." A period, a semicolon, or a dash will work.

• Don't use unnecessary commas. For instance, don't put a comma between the subject and verb of a sentence, as in the following:

No: The desk that Mike made last year, was constructed of virgin mahogany.

Yes: The desk that Mike made last year was constructed of virgin mahogany.

The following sentence can properly use commas because there is an interrupting dependent clause:

Yes: The desk, which was made in Asheville, was constructed of virgin mahogany.

But this sentence can also *not* employ commas, thereby taking on a different meaning.

Yes: The desk which was made in Asheville was constructed of virgin mahogany.

This sentence distinguishes this desk, made in Asheville, from some other desk, made elsewhere. Compare:

> The boy who loves his mother went to church.

> The boy, who loves his mother, went to church.

The first sentence makes a general statement: the sort of boy who loves his mother went to church. I can imagine someone saying this to characterize those boys who love their mothers and those who don't. The second statement is specific: a particular boy, who loves his mother, did a particular thing—attended church.

- A comma is not needed before a parenthesis:

No: The new dress shop has been doing a booming business, (although Ada refuses to visit it) but it is in a poor location.

It is okay to put a comma after a parenthesis if the sentence structure allows it—that is, if a comma would be used if the parenthesis were not there.

Yes: The new dress shop has been doing a booming business (although Ada refuses to visit it), but it is in a poor location.

In other words, a parenthesis is ignored for purposes of punctuation. When a parenthesis ends a sentence, the period goes after the parenthesis; otherwise, the parenthetical material would hang in between sentences, not attached to anything:

No: We went to the game. (it was bad) Afterward, we had dinner. (even worse)

Yes: We went to the game (very bad). Afterward, we had dinner (even worse).

If the parenthetical material is a complete thought and does stand alone, then it can stand apart from other sentences and have its ending punctuation within the parenthesis:

Yes: We went to the game. (It was very bad.) Afterward, we had dinner. (It was even worse.)

Semicolon

A light wind blew up from the southwest so that the farmers were mildly hopeful of a good rain before long; but fog and rain do not go together.

—John Steinbeck

A semicolon separates, indicating to the reader "stop; a new construction begins here; make sense of what you've just read; something else is coming now." Where you could use a period to separate sentences, you can also use a semicolon if the sentences are, in your judgment, too closely related to be separated by a period. With a semicolon, you can tell the reader to see two independent clauses together, while maintaining their distinctness as independent clauses. Steinbeck, in the sentence above, could have used a comma. But the semicolon signals a stronger pause, a stop, increasing the impact of the second sentence. The second sentence isn't a continuation of the first but rather its reversal, so Steinbeck stops the reader to set us up for that turn. A period, or a dash, or perhaps even a colon would also have been correct: in this case, as in many others, punctuation is not just a matter of correctness, but a tool of communication.

If the two clauses are complex, perhaps containing internal punctuation, then a semicolon is usually a good idea.

The ancient Egyptians built many stunning monuments; they did not build an impressive legal system respecting human rights, or administering justice openly, or applying the law consistently to all men and women.

Use semicolons to clarify sentences with conjunctive adverbs or transitional phrases. Look at these sentences:

You say we have done nothing. The Task Force has done some study, however.

These sentences make sense. The "however" indicates that the second statement contrasts with the earlier statement. Compare these sentences:

You say we have done nothing. The Task Force has done some study, however, it is not finished.

This sentence may mean either of two things:

1. I contradict your statement because the Task Force has done some study, and they are not finished yet. They are continuing to do something.
2. I agree that we have done nothing because even though the Task Force has done some study, it has not finished. Nothing has been done.

The confusion arises because the reader does not know how "however" fits into the sentence. Does "however" go with "The Task Force has done some study," or with "it is not finished"? A semicolon would make the meaning clear:

You say we have done nothing. The Task Force has done some study, however; it is not finished.

Or:

You say we have done nothing. The Task Force has done some study; however, it is not finished.

"Therefore," "moreover," and other transitional words call for a semicolon rather than just a comma:

> We want to win the tournament; therefore, we must get some sleep.

Semicolons can also be used to separate items in a series if the items are complex:

> Our plumber used his rasp, the destroyer of solid wood; his hammer, the denter of cabinet finishes; and his flashlight, the seemingly innocent (but deceptively hard-edged) scratcher of laminate finishes.

Colon

> *Hit's big as a courthouse*, he thought quietly, with a surge of peace and joy whose reason he could not have thought into words, being too young for that: *They are safe from him. People whose lives are a part of this peace and dignity are beyond his touch, he no more to them than a buzzing wasp: capable of stinging for a little moment but that's all. . . . ;*
>
> —William Faulkner

Whereas the comma says "pause," and the semicolon says "stop and separate," the colon says "go on, look ahead, here comes something." What follows a colon illustrates or explains what came before the colon. Most people are aware that a colon can introduce a list. But a colon can really introduce just about anything: a quotation, a sentence, even a word. You can see how a single word can be introduced in this sentence: now.

You also want to use a colon after the salutation in a formal letter:

> Dear Mr. Brown:

Never use a semicolon after a salutation; but do use a comma if it's an informal, friendly letter.

Also, use a colon between a title and subtitle.

Sometimes colons are incorrectly used in the middle of a sentence. The following sentence is *incorrect:* "We had planned lots of things, including: a trip to the zoo, a doctor's visit, and a workout in the gym."

End Punctuation

You know, I'm sure, that sentences generally end with a period, but you can also choose an exclamation mark or a question mark. But be very reluctant to use exclamation marks: they're the equivalent of shouting or saying "Hey! Look at me!" You occasionally want to yell at someone, but very rarely. Question marks can also go in the middle of a sentence when there is an interrogative element. Here's an example:

> Is there anyone alive? was the question running through everyone's mind.

Quotation Marks

Probably the main problem with quotation marks is knowing where to put them. Put periods and commas inside quotation marks, and put semicolons and colons outside. When you have a quotation within a quotation, use single quotation marks and double quotation marks, like this:

> Ross Perot said, "To quote a famous President, 'I cannot tell a lie.' "

Apostrophes

One job of the apostrophe is to show possession. Or, to illustrate, the apostrophe's job is to show possession. If the possessing noun is singular, just add an apostrophe and an *s* (as in the previous sentence). If the noun is plural, add only the apostrophe: the horses' stable (plural); the horse's stable (singular).

- Personal pronouns are an exception: you don't add an apostrophe to show the possessive form of personal pronouns.

  Our car is better than yours. Ours is working.

- Also, if the singular noun ends in *s*, then you may use only the apostrophe, not adding another *s*, if that sounds okay:

  The fans foolishly believed it was Coach Woods' fault.

- Finally, apostrophes can be used to show that part of a word or number has been omitted:

  '57 Chevy; I can't bear to write out "cannot."

Dashes

As a member of PONY (Prostitutes of New York), I was to spend a day on campus retreating from one role—discreet Manhattan call girl—into another: distinguished visiting prostitute.

—Tracy Quan

Some handbooks will tell you, as one prominent one puts it, that "dashes should be used sparingly in college writing." What does "sparingly" mean? Many excellent, widely published writers use dashes freely—they are, after all, extremely versatile, lively, powerful marks of punctuation. So why should you use them sparingly? The advice seems similar to saying "pitchers should use curve balls sparingly." Sure, if you threw a curve ball every play, then hitters would get used to it, ruining its effectiveness. And if you used a dash in every sentence, its impact would be dissipated. The key, it seems to me, is to use dashes effectively and judiciously. But you need to be aware that some teachers and readers are not comfortable with dashes, and find out (if at all possible) how your reader feels about them.

Here are some uses of the dash along with examples:

- Dashes can be used to insert material into a sentence—at the beginning, in the middle, at the end (as in this one). Here are sentences illustrating the two other options:

  At the beginning, in the middle, at the end—dashes can be used to insert material into a sentence.

  Dashes can be used—at the beginning, in the middle, at the end—to insert material into a sentence.

Any construction that could be put in parentheses can also be put inside dashes. Dashes are more dramatic, calling attention to the material, whereas parentheses suggest that the information inside is supplementary, or an aside.

Other Marks

Slashes.   Use slashes to indicate options or pairs: "It was a boy-meets-girl/return-of-Godzilla movie." "It was an either/or situation."

Parentheses.   Use parentheses to add information or commentary (like this). Note that the punctuation comes after the closing parenthesis, unless the parenthetical material is a complete sentence that is meant to stand alone. (There are sentences like that.) What's inside the parentheses is seen as nonessential. Whereas dashes draw attention to material, parentheses tend to downplay the material, although parenthetical remarks can also be used like whispers or afterthoughts (oh yes), which oftentimes convey the most interesting information.

Ellipses.   Ellipsis points indicate that something has been omitted. You do not need to use ellipses if it is obvious you are quoting only part of a text. For instance:

William Price Fox told the interviewer that he "didn't like to think very much before writing."

It's clear that the quoted material is just part of what Fox said. Ellipses let the reader know that material has been omitted when the reader would otherwise be unable to tell:

William Price Fox told the interviewer that he "didn't like to think . . . before writing."

Ellipses should be positioned with a space before the first dot, between each dot, and after the last dot. To show that the end of sentence has been omitted, just add another dot to the ellipses. That extra dot functions as the period of the sentence.

William Price Fox told the interviewer that he "didn't like to think . . . ."

Brackets. Brackets have two functions: to insert clarifying material into quotations, making clear that the insertion is not part of the quotation; and to serve as parentheses inside of parentheses.

William Price Fox told the interviewer that he "didn't like to think very much [about his plots] before writing."

We felt very good (the report said, after all, "there was a profit" [page 7]).

Other Conventions

Hyphens

Most teachers and editors prefer that you *not* divide words at the end of a line, so if you're using a word processing program that automatically hyphenates, turn the hyphenation off. (You should also turn off the feature that lines up the right-hand margin: although the page may look neater with the right-hand margin "justified," funny-looking spaces are often left within the line.)

• *Compound adjectives.* When you use two or more words together as an adjective modifying a noun, hyphenate the words if they come before the noun:

> Deion Sanders is a well-known athlete.
>
> As an athlete, Deion Sanders is well known.
>
> The feminist movement has affected middle-class values.
>
> The feminist movement has affected the values of the middle class.

A string of modifiers can be used for comic or ironic effect. Nora Ephron is a master of the hyphenated adjective. See, for instance, her classic essay, "A Few Words About Breasts" (in *Crazy Salad*). One example to illustrate:

> "I had those go-down-to-the-school-nurse-and-lie-on-the-cot cramps."

• *Compound Nouns.* A few compound nouns (made by putting two nouns together) are hyphenated: "mother-in-law" and "city-state," for instance. Most compound nouns are either written together or as separate words. You'll just have to check your dictionary and also consider if hyphens are necessary to make your meaning clear. There is a large difference between a sold-out house and a sold out-house. As a general rule, the only compound nouns hyphenated are those made up of equally important nouns.

• *Fractions.* When you use fractions as adjectives, hyphenate:

> We saw a one-third decrease in earnings in the last quarter.

Don't hyphenate if the fraction is used as a noun:

One third of our earnings went down the tube in the last quarter.

• *Compound Numbers.* Hyphenate numbers from twenty-one to ninety-nine:

One hundred twenty-nine people have won the Florida lottery.

• *Prefixes and Suffixes.* Hyphenate prefixes and suffixes only to avoid confusion. For instance, "re-count," as in "to re-count the money," needs to be distinguished from "recount," as in "she wanted to recount the entire story." Otherwise, if the prefix or suffix is clear, do not hyphenate.

Abbreviations

There are a few occasions when abbreviations are acceptable in formal writing, but generally you should avoid them. It's conventional to abbreviate designations before names: "Mr. Gerrn," "Mrs. Watermark," "Rev. Cloud." But "President Reagan" or "Professor Griffin" or most other designations should be spelled out. Many agency names are also commonly abbreviated, often without periods: CIA, YMCA, NCAA, and such. Do spell out the names of cities, states, countries (except, of course, in addresses); do spell out names of people and companies, unless the abbreviations are the preferred form (IBM, NCR, for example; but "Brooks Brothers" rather than "Brooks Bros."). And spell out measures ("quarts" instead of "qts." for instance).

The reason most things are spelled out is quite simple: abbreviations can be unclear. Does "23 pts." means twenty-three patients or twenty-three payments (or maybe even two three-point plays)?

Some abbreviations for Latin terms are commonly used, and you should know what they mean. But don't use them too often (especially "etc."). Use English when you can.

c.	means "about," as in "c. 1870" (about 1870)
cf.	means "compare," as in "cf. L. Lindstedt" (compare to Lindstedt)
e.g.	"for example"
etc.	"and so forth" (note that "and etc." would mean "and and so forth")
i.e.	"that is"
viz.	"namely"

Numbers

The rules for numbers are a bit numerous.

In general, spell out numbers if they can be written with one or two words: eleven, forty-two. Also spell out the number if it begins the sentence, or rewrite the sentence to avoid beginning with the number. Some exceptions:

Use numbers for fractions and decimals: 8.7, 1/2

Use numbers for hours if A.M. and P.M. are used, and for dates.

Use numbers if a sentence has a series of numbers.

If you have two numbers together, spell out the first: "He kicked two 50-yard field goals."

Italics, Underlining

In printed texts, the titles of books and other major works (musical compositions, paintings, television shows, newspapers, long poems, ships, and other things) are printed in italics, drawing attention to them as formal names. It's a convention. On your typewriter or printer, it is probably inconvenient to use italics, so most people in manuscripts use underlining to indicate italics.

You can also underline words for emphasis (<u>yes</u>, for emphasis).

And you can underline words or letters being used <u>as</u> words or letters:

The word <u>bonkers</u> really appeals to me.

Myths and Rules

Some Myths

• *Avoid "I."* I can imagine how this "rule" first occurred to some well-intentioned grammarian: Having read essays by adolescents for hours and hours, and having determined that the students seemed to be interested only in themselves, this poor teacher decides to forbid the use of "I" as a way to get the students to talk about something else. Or perhaps, after reading hundreds of sentences that began "I think," a teacher decided "Enough! I know you think it" (or rather "One knows you think it") because you are saying it. In the future, avoid 'I.'" Still, although one can sympathize with the rule inventors, one can also see that the rule is silly.

The overuse of "I" is what we want to avoid—saying "I" when saying "I" is unnecessary. Good writers use "I" all the time. Even scientific papers often use first-person pronouns—usually "we" since most scientific work has multiple authors. It often sounds stilted to say "this writer believes," "in the view of this commentator" (which may be good for comic effect). And there's absolutely nothing wrong with saying "I" if you really mean "I." Unless, of course, your teacher forbids it, in which case you may want to ask your teacher about what I'm saying here, or get John Trimble's *Writing with Style* and ask your teacher about what Trimble says.

• *Avoid "you."* The problem with "you" is that sometimes writers don't really mean "you, the reader." Rather, they mean something more specific but use "you" as a vague substitute for what they really mean. Consider this sentence from an essay about what goes on at a basketball game.

The cheerleaders just want you to yell.

Since some of the writer's readers may never have attended a basketball game, "you" can't really refer to them. The use of "they" as a vague reference is similarly problematic. Just make sure you really mean "you," and your reader can tell who "they" are.

• *Don't use contractions.* Using contractions makes your writing sound informal, more like conversation than a formal essay. Throughout this section I've used contractions because an informal, friendly tone is exactly what I want. But in much academic writing, you really want to sound more formal; and in many work situations, especially in business letters and legal documents, you probably want to restrict carefully the use of contractions. Robert Connors and Andrea Lunsford, in the instructor's edition of their fine *St. Martin's Handbook*, offer this illuminating observation:

> Fred Astaire would have sounded somewhat stiff singing "Is it not romantic?" while Abraham Lincoln would have struck an incongruously chatty tone had he said, "With firmness in the right, as God gives us to see the right, let's strive on to finish what we're in." (p. 479)

Even in formal situations, sometimes a contraction may be right, especially if the alternative sounds stilted or pretentious. When in doubt, however, you should probably err on the side of formality. You just have to consider your audience, your goal, the persona you put forward, the content of your essay. Such decision making is more difficult than simply following an injunction against contractions; but it's also more effective.

• *Avoid starting a sentence with "And" or "But."* Good writers start sentences with "And" and "But" all the time. There is no valid reason why learning writers shouldn't have access to this effective strategy.

So why is this rule so popular? Perhaps, again, because some teachers have been uncomfortable with informality, and such sentence beginnings do sound like a human being talking. Some of the most formal prose in our language, however, includes such beginnings. Sounding like a person talking on paper—if that talking person sounds articulate and intelligent—is not a liability. By no means. Obviously, you don't want to sound chatty or chummy, and you want to be careful not to overuse "But" and "And." (Indeed, you want to avoid overusing any device.) You want to use a variety of sentence structures and not just string simple sentences together with "And" and "But."

Given those cautions, begin sentences with "And" and "But" whenever you feel such openings will help your writing flow and enhance the conversational tone.

• *Don't write a very long or very short paragraph.* This is another superstition not supported by any extensive examination of what good writers do. Variety in paragraph length is refreshing. Of course, variety for variety's sake is not ideal, and you do want the length of your paragraphs to reflect the ideas they contain. Very short paragraphs are dramatic, interrupting the flow, standing out, moving a bit faster. Very long paragraphs are useful, obviously, for working through a complex idea, for staying with a line of thought, for extending a meditation. Let your ideas and the effect you're trying to create determine the length of your paragraphs—not some arbitrary rule.

• *Begin every paragraph with a topic sentence.* In 1974 Richard Braddock conducted a study of "The Frequency and Placement of Topic Sentences" by examining how professional writers actually use topic sentences. Braddock concluded that the usual textbook advice to begin every paragraph with a topic sentence is not supported by the evidence. Braddock found that less than a fifth of those experienced writers' paragraphs contained topic sentences. (See *Research in the Teaching of English* 8 [Winter 1974]: 287–302.)

What does this finding mean for you? Certainly you want your reader to be able to follow your logic. But there may be advantages to arguing your point in a particular paragraph without stating directly what that point is. Just presenting the evidence may convince a reader in the way that an assertion plus the same evidence would not. Also, paragraphs are often building on a point expressed in an earlier or later paragraph. Essays apparently come in chunks that may range over more than one paragraph.

On the other hand, basing his argument on work in psycholinguistics, Frank D'Angelo has asserted that topic sentences do make prose easier to read, allowing readers to process information more efficiently ("The Topic Sentence Revisited," *College English* 37 [1986]: 431–41). So, if your goal is simply to convey information, topic sentences may be of more value. If you're conducting an argument, I suggest you think about what you want to say and how you want to affect the reader, and not worry about whether every paragraph has a topic sentence.

• *Use specific and concrete language.* There is nothing inherently good or bad about either general or specific, concrete or abstract language. Some older handbooks and style guides told students to "use specific and concrete language" in an effort, understandably, to get students to avoid vague and imprecise language. But general and abstract terms are essential to writers: without them, we cannot speak in general or abstract terms! A writer may well want to talk about the deployment of Napolean's small artillery at the battle of Waterloo; but a writer may also want to talk about "war" in general, in the abstract.

What we find in good writing is a mixture of the specific/concrete and the abstract/general. Movement back and forth is effective, from assertion to evidence or vice versa. So, if you want to talk about "the car," that's fine: just include some concrete discussion. And if you want to talk about the windshield-wiper design on your blue 1983 Honda Civic, that's fine too: just include some reference to the general big picture.

• *Never use passive voice.* Do use passive voice if you want to emphasize the passivity of the subject: "He was struck by a train while sitting on his front porch." Or if the agent of an action is unknown or unimportant: "The test tube was filled with nitrogen." Otherwise, prefer active voice unless you have some other reason for using passive.

• *Never shift verb tenses.* What is important is to keep the reader oriented in time. It's when the reader can't tell what the author's point of view is that verb tense becomes important. Even a sentence can have several tenses if the writer's stance is clear.

Confusing stance:	She told her mother that he speaks to her when he was dying.
Clear stance:	She told her mother that he had spoken to her when he was dying.
Clear stance with multiple tenses:	She will tell her parents that you have been the one who sits there.

Some Rules

Although there probably are not any rules that always apply, these are pretty solid. Most have been discussed previously in this guide and will just be reviewed here.

• *Avoid ambiguous or misleading fragments.* Sentence fragments are groups of words that are incorrectly used as sentences. Sometimes these fragments take the form of a subordinate (or dependent) clause, which merely modifies another clause and cannot stand on its own. Other times, the fragments lack subjects or verbs that would allow them to stand on their own. A good way to find sentence fragments in your reading is by reading each sentence aloud. If each sentence is not a complete thought, if your reader, hearing only that sentence would go "Huh?" then it is most likely a fragment. Thus: "The boys in the band" is a fragment, and should be changed to something like, "We are the boys in the band."

• *Distinguish correctly between* it's *and* its. The confusion of the words *it's* and *its* is one of the most common mistakes in student writing. *Its* is a personal pronoun, just like "our" and "their." It is used in sentences where an object is being talked about:

John just built a birdhouse. Its orange roof can be seen three blocks away.

In this sentence "its" replaces the word "birdhouse" in the second sentence, thus acting as a pronoun.

It's, on the other hand, is a contraction of the verb phrase "it is." Contractions are often used in informal writing, less often in formal papers. When using *it's,* be sure you have a verb, not a pronoun:

Have you every tried to fly a plane? It's fun.

• *Punctuate correctly the end of complete thoughts.* You can end a complete thought with a comma only if a connecting word like "and" or "but" and another complete thought follows. You can also end a complete thought with a semicolon if another complete thought follows. You can use a colon followed by a complete thought, a list, a phrase, or a single word. Don't connect complete thoughts with just a comma.

• *Don't shift tenses unnecessarily.* (See "Verbs," pages 121–127.)

• *Use an apostrophe for possessives.* (See "Apostrophe," pages 134–135.)

• *A comma connects; a semicolon separates.* (See "Comma" and "Semicolon," pages 127–133.)

• *Make pronoun references clear.* When you use "he," "she," or any pronoun, make sure the reader can easily discern the reference. "This" by itself is often obscure to readers; it's a good idea to avoid using "this" alone and instead just to say "this concept," "this actor," this whatever.

• *Watch out for modifiers that dangle.* Here's an example of a dangling modifier:

Flying low, cows were seen downtown.

The phrase "flying low" is not attached to any noun. Obviously it was intended to modify some agent who observed cows downtown by flying low. But because the phrase isn't attached, and is "dangling," it naturally appears to apply to (or modify) the nearest noun: cows. So it sounds as if the cows were flying low. (Which could be pretty bad!) The problem is easily corrected: just make sure modifiers have the right agent expressed. Usually you'll find dangling modifiers hanging out at the beginning of sentences, and sometimes at the end. Here are a couple more examples so you can get used to spotting them:

Excitedly, the sports car was purchased at a modest price.
(Was the sports car excited? Seems unlikely.)

Selected for teaching ability, the scholarship of professors actually becomes more important.
(The scholarship wasn't selected.)

• ***Make sure sentence elements agree.*** Subjects and verbs, nouns and pronouns need to agree. Problems with subjects and verbs often arise when these elements are separated, so in proofreading pay particular attention to complex sentences.

• ***Use the right preposition.*** Prepositions are often tricky. We say we saw something "on" television, but "at" the movies. In English, the right preposition for a particular use is often a matter of convention. If you're uncomfortable with Standard English, you'll just have to learn which preposition to use. You'll find the *Oxford Advanced Learner's Dictionary* to be particularly helpful on prepositions.

• ***Use the right word.*** At some point your teacher will probably write "diction" or just "d" in the margin of a paper. You may have already encountered such a comment. On the one hand, it may mean that the words you choose seem not to fit the level of the paper. See if your diction might be too informal or casual, or perhaps too stuffy. On the other hand, such a comment may mean that the word doesn't mean quite what your teacher thinks you want it to mean. Look it up: a good dictionary will help you distinguish the meaning as well as the usual context of the word and also will help you pick another word.

• ***Place quotation marks correctly.*** Notice where periods, commas, colons, and semicolons go.

"Like this."

"Like this," he said.

"Like this": yes, he said it again with a colon.

He said, "Like this"; she asked, "Like this?"

Did he say, "Do it like this"?

This Is the Name of the Book

This is the first sentence of the book; I can see already that you are beginning to be disappointed. You are thinking that the second sentence of this book had better do something clever, or you're outa here. But you're not really a person of your word, or perhaps that wasn't really your word: you already can see this is the third sentence of this book. This very short book has the wrong title—it's really about punctuation, illustrating commas, semicolons, colons, and dashes.

A Few Common Errors

• **accept, except.** This sentence illustrates the difference in these two words, often confused:

The Congress voted to accept the treaty except for the final provision.

Remember, *except* means "an exception."

• **affect, effect.** *Affect* is usually a verb meaning "to influence":

The election affects everyone.

Effect is usually a noun meaning "the result":

The effects of the election will be profound.

Less commonly, *affect* is used by psychologists as a noun to mean "emotional state":

The teenager had a depressed affect.

And *effect* is also less commonly used to mean "bring about":

The budget reductions will effect huge unemployment.

- **ain't.** In most contexts, *ain't* isn't acceptable.

- **all right, alright.** Many people use *alright* but *all right is* correct; *alright* isn't. Remember it this way: *alright* misspells "all"; therefore, it's wrong. *All right* spells both words correctly: it's right. All right?

- **alot, a lot.** Use *a lot,* not *alot.* Like *all right,* the two-word version is correct. Some readers feel that *a lot,* even if it is spelled correctly, is very casual, shaky in formal writing. Consider using something else if it will work as well.

- **among.** See *between.*

- **as.** See *like.*

- **assure, ensure, insure.** Use *assure* to talk about making a person certain:

I want to assure you I am ready.

Use *ensure* to talk about objects or actions:

I want to ensure the brakes will work.

Use *insure* with regard to finances and insurance:

I want to insure my house against falling frozen turkeys.

- **bad, badly.** *Bad* is an adjective, *badly* an adverb:

She sang so badly the audience felt bad.

In that sentence, *badly* modifies the verb "sang"; *bad* modifies the noun "audience."

- **between.** The general rule is to use *between* for two persons or things, and use *among* for more than two:

The feud between Jake and the Fatman is over.

The feud among the networks is over.

But you can use *between* for more than two if a close relationship is intended.

• **bring.** See *take.*

• **can, may.** Although the distinction seems a bit fussy to some, *can* refers to an ability:

Can he ski?

asks whether he is able. *May* refers to permission:

May he ski?

requests permission.

• **cannot.** Although *cannot* is preferred, *can not is* also acceptable if special emphasis on "not" is desired.

• **center on, center around.** Many authorities believe *center on* should be used instead of *center around.*

• **conscious, conscience.** *Conscious* means awareness; *conscience* refers to the moral sense.

• **consensus.** There's no need to say "consensus of opinion" or "general consensus" because *consensus* means "the shared opinion." So "consensus of opinion" says literally "the shared opinion of opinion."

• **continual, continuous.** A *continual* process is repeated regularly. A continuous process is ongoing, without interruption.

- **criterion, criteria.** *Criterion* is singular:

We judge beauty contestants by only one criterion.

Criteria is plural and therefore, obviously, shouldn't be used for only one standard:

We judge beauty contestants by many criteria.

- **data.** Though originally a plural noun (the singular is *datum)*, the word *data* can be used as either a plural or a singular noun. The plural form is most often found in the fields of research and statistics.

- **different from, different than.** Many people feel *different from* sounds better: most usage guides say something like "generally preferred in formal writing." You may find, however, when a long clause follows, that *different than* sounds better.

- **disinterested, uninterested.** You would probably want to be judged by a "disinterested jury," because *disinterested* means they would have no prejudice, no special interests in the case. An "uninterested jury" would be likely not to pay close attention, because *uninterested* means having no interest, being bored.

- **ensure.** See *assure.*

- **etc.** This abbreviation stands for *et cetera,* Latin for "and so forth." Thus, "and etc." literally says "and and so forth." Just put a comma before *etc.,* without an "and":

We want hot dogs, cole slaw, french fries, etc.

- **farther, further.** *Farther* is used with physical distance, *further* with abstract concepts.

You travel farther down the road; you try to further your career.

• **first, firstly.** *Firstly* appears in British English (along with *secondly, thirdly,* and so on). For an American audience, use *first, second, third,* and so on. You may also use numbers in parentheses: (1), (2), and (3).

• **flammable, inflammable.** Though these two words sound and look like opposites, they are in fact synonyms.

• **good, well.** Don't use *good* as a substitute for the adverb *well:*

The team played well (not "good").

• **imply, infer.** Speakers or authors *imply;* listeners or readers *infer.* To imply something is to hint at it, to suggest it rather than say it directly. To infer is to receive the meaning, to figure it out. The words mean, in other words, very different things: one is passing on, giving; the other is taking in, receiving.

• **inflammable.** See *flammable.*

• **insure.** See *assure.*

• **irregardless.** Although sometimes people say *irregardless* is not a word, obviously it is one: there it is. But it is not a good word, by most people's standards: it means simply "regardless," so why add the useless *ir-?*

• **its, it's.** *It's* means "it is." *Its* is the possessive pronoun. The problem is that possessive forms usually have an apostrophe: Steve's, Mary's, the team's. But note that *hers, yours, ours,* and *theirs* do not take an apostrophe. *Its* works the same way in the possessive, allowing *it's* to stand for the contraction of "it is." You might try thinking of it this way: with *its,* the s belongs to the *it*—it is possessive. With *it's,* the apostrophe marks a space where something is missing, namely the *i* in *is.*

• **lay, lie.** The verb *to lie* is used when there is no object:

I will lie on the ground.

To lay is used when there is an object:

I will lay my books on the ground.

(Of course, the issue is muddied by the fact that the past tense of *lie* is *lay*. But that's another story. See page 125.)

• **like, as, as if.** When trying to decide whether to use *like* or *as,* check to see if a verb follows. If it doesn't, then use *like,* which functions like a preposition:

He wanted a friend like his dad's.

If a verb does follow, then use *as,* which can function like a preposition or a conjunction leading to a clause:

He wanted a friend, as every man wants one.

Here's an example:

The doctor worked like a machine, as if she were possessed by some healing spirit.

• **loan.** There is some disagreement about the use of this word as a verb, in place of the word *lend.* Many would say that it is technically correct; however, many others could be found who would disagree strongly. Since one of these latter might be your instructor, it's probably best to use *lend* instead, reserving *loan* for use as a noun.

• **loose, lose.** *Loose* means "not attached." *Lose* means "to come to be without something." For example:

If you keep your keys loose you may lose one.

- **may.** See *can.*

- **media.** This is a plural noun; its singular is *medium.* It is incorrect to say "The media is . . . " unless you're working in the very specialized world of advertising, in which the singular form is usually considered acceptable.

- **none.** *None* can be either singular or plural, depending on the noun that follows:

> None of the park has been renovated.

> None of the children were playing.

If there is no noun following, then decide yourself whether you mean *none* of a single thing or *none* of two or more.

- **only.** This word causes trouble if it isn't placed next to what it modifies. Notice the difference in these two sentences:

> Professor Grumpy gives C's only to those students he doesn't know.

> Professor Grumpy gives only C's to those students he doesn't know.

The first sentence says that only those unknown students will get C's: everyone else will get some other grade. The second sentence says that those unknown students can only get C's: that's the highest grade they'll get.

- **people, persons.** Though it is a rule not strictly followed, the use of *persons* is preferred when a particular number is being specified:

> This elevator carries a maximum load of 15 persons.

• **precede.** *Precede* means to come before, but it is often mis-spelled because it sounds like *proceed.* But the two are spelled differently, as you can see.

• **principal, principle.** A *principle* is a truth, a rule, an idea. This word is always a noun. *Principal* means "the leader," "the chief official," "the money invested or loaned." As an adjective, *principal* means "the chief," "the most significant." If you remember that the school princi*pal* is your "pal," you can keep these two straight.

• **reason, because.** Many writers think it is necessary to use both of these words in the same sentence, but it is redundant. Instead of "The reason he left is because the food was gone," say "He left because the food was gone," or "The reason he left is that the food was gone."

• **shall, will.** Today we use *will* in almost every situation, but decades ago a distinction was made: I *shall,* we *shall,* you *will,* they *will,* he/she/it *will.* "I shall" and "we shall" sound very stuffy and fussy to most people, although *shall* can be used for emphasis:

He shall come at four o'clock or he's fired.

• **take, bring.** Correct choice depends on the speaker's location.

I take an object to another location; you bring an object to my location.

• **their, they're, there.** Most writers know what they should use when they misuse these words, but it is difficult to keep the mistake from showing up in papers. Remember the correct usage of these words and double-check for them.

Their word is not reliable; they're going to build the office right there on the nature preserve.

- **therefore.** *Therefore* can be used in place of the word *so:*

I passed the final examination; so I will pass the class.

I passed the final examination; therefore I will pass the class.

The two words should not be used together, as this is redundant:

I passed the final examination; so therefore I will pass the class.

- **uninterested.** See *disinterested.*

- **unique.** All the handbooks say that "very unique" makes no sense. Personally, it makes perfect sense to me:

A man with purple hands is unique; a man with eleven purple hands that flash Morse code is very unique, in my opinion.

But almost everyone else will think "very unique" is poor usage.

- **used to, use to.** Use *used to.* In speech the final *d* tends not to be heard, but it should be retained:

I used to go there every Friday.

- **who's, whose.** *Whose is* possessive; *who's* is the contraction for "who is." For example:

Who's going to find out whose car was hit?

- **would of, would have.** Use *would have. Would of* is a decayed version, an error based on what "would have" sounds like when some people say it. *Have* should also follow *could, should, might.*

• **your, you're.** *You're* is the contraction for "you are." *Your* is possessive. For example:

You're not in your right mind.

6

Research and Documentation

Read not to contradict and confute; nor to believe and take for granted; not to find talk and discourse; but to weigh and consider.

—Sir Francis Bacon

The key to a successful research paper is *controlling* your information, not just reporting it. You can begin to exert this control before you've actually begun gathering data. Simply take the time to write down whatever you know about the topic before you start searching. This pre-research inventory not only gives you a clearer idea of what you already know and what you need to know, but also may suggest lines of research that would be overlooked later, by a more "informed" perspective. Writing before researching may also give you a better sense of your writing task: if you've given some thought to your audience, your purpose, and your presentation, you'll likely have a better sense of which data will be most useful for your purpose. But writing a research paper is like writing anything else—your purpose will probably evolve as you work.

Finding Sources

When you're ready to do research, keep in mind that the library may not be your only resource. If you're doing research on John F. Kennedy's foreign policy, for instance, you just might have a parent or uncle who was alive when Kennedy was president. If you're really lucky, perhaps your uncle took part in the Bay of Pigs "invasion" or had some other relevant experience. At any rate, recognize that conducting your own interviews, experiments, and observations may provide you with some excellent data, information that might not even be available in the library. Such first-hand information is called a "primary" source; "secondary" sources are works one step removed from the source. For instance, a speech by Kennedy about his foreign policy would be considered a primary source; a scholarly book about Kennedy's policy would be a secondary source.

When you do actually get to the library, don't hesitate to ask for help. Reference librarians supposedly like to help people use the library—that's usually why they became reference librarians. If the library offers tours or introductions, take advantage, unless you're already an informed user: the time invested will pay off.

Although an introduction to using the Internet and its vast resources is beyond our scope here, most libraries can provide assistance, if you're not already surfing the Net. A search service, like Yahoo or Magellan or Excite, can sift through thousands of data bases and locate information on whatever topics you designate. Such search services, once you're logged on, provide explanations of how to use them effectively. Your biggest problem will likely be figuring out how to examine all the material that a search uncovers.

If the library's card catalogue is on-line, you can look sources up a little faster, and you may be able to search by "key words" in addition to searching by author, title, or subject. An on-line catalogue is also likely to let you know if the book is already checked out, and if so, when it is due back. But an old-fashioned card system will work just fine, and doesn't go off-line.

Let's imagine you have a rather vague notion that you want to write a research paper on Eudora Welty's career. As you search through works on Welty, here's a sample of what you'd see on the screen or the card:

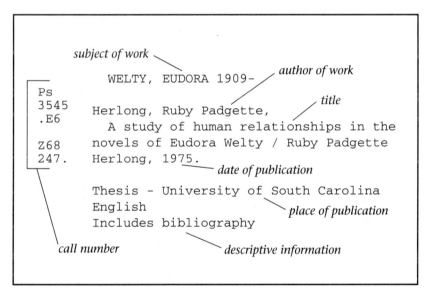

✦ **Figure 6.1**   Sample Screen on Electronic Card Catalogue

Is this a work you should consult? For most research topics and most libraries, there will be vastly more material than you can handle. So you'll need to evaluate the available resources, considering the following aspects:

1. Does the work promise to shed any light on your topic? Yes, it appears to be on Welty's novels, which is certainly part of the topic at this point.

2. Does the work appear to be an important or well-known study? One measure of the importance of a work is the publisher. Although lousy books are occasionally published by major presses, and great books by minor presses, you can usually bet that a book published by a major university or commercial press has some merit. Books by such university presses as Cambridge, Oxford, Yale, Harvard, or California are almost certainly important. If you locate books related to your topic published by such major presses, you should definitely try to see them. You can also judge the quality of potential sources and learn a good deal about your topic, too, by consulting reviews of these sources—although you should also keep in mind that reviewers of books, like reviewers of movies and everything else, are certainly fallible.

The sample work, by Ruby Herlong, you will notice, is not published by a press: it is designated as a thesis completed at the University of South Carolina in 1975, which means it was a work written to satisfy the requirements for a Master's (or M.A.) degree. Although it very well may be an excellent thesis, it is not likely to be a well-known, important source; even if it were designated as a "dissertation," which is the work written for a doctoral degree, you would probably want to consider looking at other sources that have been published before investigating this one.

3. Can this source lead you to other useful sources? A very recent thesis or dissertation could provide you with the names of other works to consult, but so could a recently published article or book. Thus, unless this source offers some unique insights, you should rank it lower on your priority list, looking at it if you have time, only after you've consulted higher priority items.

If you are researching a relatively unfamiliar topic, then some sources that provide general and introductory information would be very valuable. Encyclopedia articles can be helpful in leading you to other sources, and also in letting you know what is common knowledge, although you ordinarily will not want to cite them (precisely because they do present what is widely known). Many computers now are sold with an encyclopedia on disk; while these are handy for basic information, the quality of encyclopedias varies widely. I like the *Encyclopedia Brittanica* for depth and reliabilty (I've already found two huge factual errors in the encyclopedia that came with my computer). You also need to exercise tremendous caution in using network and information-service sources: not everything on the Net is reliable. (Of course, not everything in print is reliable either.)

For British figures, the *Dictionary of National Biography* (or *DNB*) can be an invaluable background source; for American authors, consult the appropriate volume of the *Dictionary of Literary Biography* (or *DLB*). The *Atlantic Brief Lives: A Biographical Companion to the Arts* is a wonderful resource because each of the brief lives is written by an eminent scholar of that figure. And there is an *Oxford Companion* volume for almost any subject area now: for Welty, you would consult the *Oxford Companion to American Literature,* for instance.

Helpful bibliographies and indexes are likely to be available in the reference area; if so, these will be clearly designated in the card catalogue. General indexes list material found in magazines and newspapers: try the *Reader's Guide to Periodical Literature,* or the *Magazine Index,* or the *New York Times Index.* More specialized indexes, including scholarly work, cover various areas, as their titles indicate: *Humanities Index, General Science Index, Social Science Index, Monthly Catalogues of Government Publications, Business Periodicals Index,* and *Essay and General Literature Index,* to name some of the most prominent.

There are other reference works that anyone doing research should know about: the *Oxford English Dictionary,* commonly called the *OED,* the standard source regarding the history of words; the *World Almanac,* a statistical storehouse, published annually, which provides a chronology of the previous year's important events; the *Times Atlas of the World,* a five-volume treasure of maps; and Bartlett's *Familiar Quotations,* or some other quotation collection.

When you decide to examine a book or an article, its location is indicated, of course, by its call number, displayed by the card catalogue. If the work is not checked out but not on the shelf, look for the books waiting to be shelved. If you still can't find it, go to the circulation desk and request a search for the book. It's always a good idea to start as soon as possible, but the value of starting a research project as far ahead of the due date as possible should be obvious: you can't always count on materials being easily available.

Gathering Material

As you begin to gather sources and look through them, it's likely that your topic will evolve. If you were thinking of writing about Welty's career, you may quickly realize that whole books have already been written about that. Unless you have the time to write a book right now and have a new angle on the issue, you will probably decide to reconsider your topic. The more familiar you are with what has been done already, the better position you're in to decide what you might do. If you did some brainstorming before you started your research, you might refer back to it for some ideas on how to focus your paper. What aspects of Welty's career, for instance, are you most interested in? What aspects seem most promising to you?

As you read, you'll want to take notes. While actively marking up a text as you read is often helpful, you do not want to mark up a library book: to mark important passages, you may want to insert slips of paper. It is more helpful if you can assimilate what you're reading, copying down those phrases, sentences, and passages that you may want to quote later (be sure to indicate with quotation marks those passages that are copied), summarizing particular points, articulating your responses and ideas. Copy, summarize, re-flect—those are your jobs. Keep track of the sources you consult, noting somewhere the author, title, place of publication, publisher, date of publication, and call number: if you're writing on-line, go ahead and begin your bibliography in a separate file; if you're not digitized, then fill out an index card for each work with the full information.

The sooner you can focus your topic, the faster you'll be able to sort out those works you want to see and sort through the information in them. You aren't likely to have time to read through all the books you'll consult; rather, you'll be reading selectively, skimming some and skipping some. And, of course, writing down your thoughts. If you don't put your ideas on paper as you work, you'll likely lose them, unless you have a photographic memory. As you process information, occasionally take time out to brainstorm and freewrite and gather your thoughts together *on paper.* You are looking, as you research, for a controlling idea; once you have one (which will be subject to change), the paper will gather considerable momentum.

Let's imagine, for example, that as you work with material about Welty, you find yourself interested by the economic aspects of her work. You become curious about the publishing history of her work, how much money she made, how comfortable she might have been. If your research could focus on tracking her financial status, and comparing how she was doing to what she was writing, then you'd have a much better idea what research materials to look for, and how to use them. If this topic is viable, then pretty quickly you should be able to start organizing your information.

You may at some point want to construct an outline. Outlines are often helpful, especially for research papers, especially if you view them as preliminary sketches and not an iron-clad plan. Sometimes it's easier to just begin drafting, since constructing the outline would require you to think through things that you can't yet think through except by writing. If you've recorded ideas on notecards or in a computer file, you can start playing around with the order of their presentation, and how your controlling idea will pull the material together.

As you begin to select and arrange the material, it's especially crucial that you keep track of which ideas and quotations come from which sources. You want to be absolutely certain that in your finished product you give credit to your sources for their words and ideas. If you use someone else's words or ideas and fail to let the reader know, then you are committing plagiarism. The usual penalty for plagiarism ranges from failing the paper, to failing the course, to being expelled from school.

To make sure you understand what is meant by plagiarism, let's look at some examples. Here is a quotation from a work by Douglas Kimmel, called *Adulthood and Aging:*

> A second approach to studying the index of age is a longitudinal study. In this research strategy, a group of subjects is selected, appropriate for the question being studied, and is given a series of questionnaires, tests, or interviews periodically over several years.

Anyone who knows even a little about research design realizes that this statement presents what is common knowledge. It is a statement of fact available in any general introduction or encyclopedia or even dictionary. You need not cite this source if you use the general statement of fact presented here—it isn't Kimmel's idea to begin with. You could write the following, for instance, without citing Kimmel:

> Researchers choose subjects and give them tests and talk with them at different intervals over many years. This method of research is called a longitudinal study.

If you know nothing about the subject matter, however, then you'll be unable to distinguish what is common knowledge from what isn't.

If you quote any part of Kimmel's passage, then you'll have to indicate your source:

> A longitudinal study is a research strategy in which, as Douglas Kimmel says, "a group of subjects is selected, appropriate for the question being studied, and is given a series of questionnaires, tests, or interviews" at regular intervals over a long time (34).

Notice how the quoted material is introduced here by mentioning the author and how the quotation flows smoothly in the sentence. The quotation marks indicate where the quoted material begins and ends, and the page number in parentheses tells readers where to find the quoted material in the original.

If you use an idea from someone else's work, then you also must provide a citation, even if you don't actually quote the other source. Here's a passage written by Nancy Sommers, which appears on page 388 of a work on composition research:

> The experienced writers see their revision as a recursive process—a process with significant recurring activities—with different levels of attention and agenda for each cycle. During the first revision cycle their attention is primarily directed towards narrowing the topic and delimiting their ideas. At this point, they are not as concerned as they are later about vocabulary and style.

And here is a passage written by Jennie Ariail, which does not quote Sommers, but does appropriately credit her for providing the ideas:

> As Nancy Sommers reports, one of the differences between experienced and student writers is the way they approach revision. Experienced writers, Sommers says, understand that revision takes place over time, on many different levels. Usually in the first draft, she argues, these writers are trying to get their ideas down and focused (388).

Notice how clearly Ariail attributes Sommers's ideas to her. There can be no question here about which ideas belong to Sommers, and which to Ariail.

Notice also how Ariail efficiently summarizes Sommers's main point. How did she do that? A good summary does two things: it accurately conveys the essence of the original text's meaning, and it puts that meaning into the present writer's own words. A paraphrase also translates an original text into other words; unlike a summary, which gets to the heart of the original, a paraphrase tries to capture the entirety of the original, just putting it in other words.

Notice that Ariail leaves out some of Sommers's details, but she doesn't distort her meaning in getting to the bottom line. She also leaves behind Sommers's more technical terms, like "recursive" and "revision cycle," and uses instead words that her audience will more readily understand. Sommers is writing for an informed audience, and she is assuming that her readers will see the whole essay; thus, Ariail's summary makes Sommers's meaning more available to readers than Sommers's own words, taken out of context.

To produce a summary or paraphrase, in other words, you must understand the original text. Perhaps that goes without saying, yet I've often encountered summaries and paraphrases that didn't give such an impression. If you are having difficulty understanding a passage as you research (and everyone inevitably does have such trouble), here are some things to try:

1. Note the passage and come back to it later after you've read more material; it may make more sense after you have more information.
2. Make sure you understand the terms being used (dictionaries are your friends; there are even specialized dictionaries for various disciplines).
3. Talk to someone about it (an expert would be ideal, but anyone may be helpful).

4. Try to underline the main idea; circle words or phrases that mark relationship ("therefore," "if, then" "for instance"), and make sure you see the relationship.

5. Try to articulate the difficulty you're having: oftentimes by explaining a problem, you'll see a solution. Writing about a text gives you a chance to slow down your thinking, see the meanings on paper, and actively involve yourself in deciphering.

Quoting and Documenting

Why quote? It can add credibility, interest, and eloquence to your paper. Also, you may want to draw attention to the way something is said. Imagine the evening news without any film clips or correspondents: just one guy sitting in front of the camera, reading. Your quotations are in a sense like the film clips and on-the-scene correspondents: they provide other voices and firsthand evidence, enlivening and enriching your paper.

You do not, however, want to quote simply for the sake of quoting or filling your page. Quote only when you need to have someone else's actual words before the reader; otherwise, paraphrase or summarize.

There are two ways to insert quoted material into your text: as part of your sentences, and indented as a block. In either case, be sure to introduce quoted material clearly, working it smoothly into your own text. Don't just plop a quotation down: it's sort of like hearing a disembodied voice suddenly start talking; it's disorienting. Keep your reader oriented by making clear who is talking (unless you have some reason to disorient or tease the reader, of course). So there will be no question where your words end and someone else's begin, carefully mark the beginnings and ends of quoted material with quotation marks. If there is a quotation inside the quotation, use single quote marks for the inner quotation.

The quotations from Sommers and Ariail above are indented (or inset). Usually, if a quotation extends more than four lines on your page, you should indent it (one inch, ordinarily). Writers sometimes indent shorter passages in order to draw more attention to them. Since indenting the passage as a block indicates it is a quotation, don't use quotation marks to open and close it. If there is a quotation within an indented quotation, then you may use regular quotation marks to mark it.

If you need to insert a word into a quotation in order to make it grammatically correct within your sentence, then put brackets around whatever you added. If you need to leave out part of a quotation, then use ellipses (three periods with spaces) to indicate omitted material.

How do you indicate the source of a quotation? That depends on the discipline within which you're working. Different fields of study have somewhat different formats, but all of them make it possible for a reader to track down the quotation—to check your use of it, to read the entire work, to search for additional support, whatever. If you're not sure what format to use for a particular paper, ask. Essentially, there are two main ways of documenting: the footnotes method, and the works-cited method.

Footnotes

With footnotes, you put a raised number in the text itself, referring the reader to notes that are numbered at the bottom of the page, or collected at the end of the paper (which makes them, technically, endnotes). The note (foot or end) then gives the author, title, date and place of publication, and page number. Notes may also be used to comment, offering some additional explanation or argument that is for some reason not made part of the text. Using footnotes, you will still (ordinarily) need at the end a bibliography of the works you used.

Works Cited

With the works-cited form, you simply indicate the page number of a quotation in parentheses immediately following the quotation. If the author's name hasn't been indicated, then include that in parentheses also. For instance:

> Mr. Spock's most recent book explains the background of the famous Vulcan axiom, "The good of the many outweighs the good of the few, or the one" (44–49).

At the end of the paper, the reader finds a list entitled Works Cited, where the full information regarding Spock's book appears, like a bibliography. It is also possible to have notes using the works-cited format, but these are used to comment, not to document.

In a bibliography or list of works cited, include the following information for a book:

- Author's name, last name first, followed by a period and two spaces. If there are two authors, list both this way: Lynn, Steven, and Anna Lynn. If there are more than two, you can indicate there are others with "et al." (Latin for "and others").
- Title of the book (underlined), followed by a period and then two spaces.
- Place of publication, followed by a colon. Use only the city if it's familiar.
- Publisher's name, followed by a comma and a space. You may be able to abbreviate "University Press" as "UP," and "Press" as "P."
- Year of publication.

Kimmel, Douglas C. <u>Adulthood and Aging.</u> New York: John Wiley and Sons, 1990.

For journal and magazine articles, include this information:

- Author's name, last name first, followed by a period and two spaces.
- Title, in quotation marks, followed by a period (don't forget to close the quotation marks after the period) and two spaces.
- Underlined title of the magazine or journal.
- Volume number, if applicable.
- Date of publication in parentheses, followed by a colon.
- Page numbers of the article, followed by a period.

Ortez, Alfonso. "Origins." <u>National Geographic</u> (October 1991): 4–13.

For research papers in the social sciences, you are likely to be asked to use the American Psychological Association style (or APA style), which varies slightly the works-cited form described here. In the sciences, you're likely to use the *CBE Style Manual*.

Use whatever style of documentation that your instructor expects—just be sure to use one.

Index

✦ ✦ ✦

174